AF531698

Money and Markets from Pre-Colonial to Colonial India

Money and Markets from Pre-Colonial to Colonial India

Anirban Biswas

AAKAR

MONEY AND MARKETS FROM
PRE-COLONIAL TO COLONIAL INDIA
Anirban Biswas

First Published, 2007

ISBN 978-81-89833-20-6

Published by
AAKAR BOOKS
28 E Pocket IV, Mayur Vihar Phase I, Delhi-110 091
Phone : 011-2279 5505 Telefax : 011-2279 5641
aakarbooks@gmail.com; www.aakarbooks.com

Printed at
Mudrak, 30-A, Patparganj, Delhi–110 091

Dedicated to

My Teacher Late Professor Dipak Banerjee

and to

My Elder Brother Sri Basudeb Biswas

Contents

Foreword

I got to know Sri Anirban Biswas when he was a postgraduate student of the Department of Economics, Calcutta University. I had already known of him from his writings in different journals, including the *Frontier.* Meeting him, I was impressed by his curiosity on many aspects of society and the social sciences. A few years after doing his M.A., Anirban chose to go to a college situated at a village in a south Bengal district. The distance from the city life of Calcutta, now Kolkata, could not, however, smother his quest for learning. Economic history has been one of his favourite subjects, and he began to study the monetary and commercial history of India and Europe, whenever time permitted, since the early 1990s. In 2005, he produced a monograph that brought to light a neglected but interesting aspect of Indian monetary history. This monograph, I have come to learn, has attracted the attention of scholars and I myself have found it very much interesting. Writing such a monograph can, I think, be considered an achievement on the part of one who lives at a village and is in constant struggle with paucity of resources, as well as with a considerable teaching load.

The canvas of the present study is wider. In this, Anirban has discussed the pre-colonial monetary economy of India in general and Bengal in particular, and has provided an account of the transitional phase in Bengal and Eastern India that started with the arrival of the British rulers. What I find particularly interesting is his attempt to correlate monetary transition with other institutional changes, and to describe the conflicts within various areas of the economy. He has relied mainly on secondary and printed primary sources. I think this deficiency has been adequately made up for by economic analyses of the data he has collated from these sources. Anirban has demonstrated a reasonably good command of the standard tools of economic theory and a familiarity with a wide range of scholarly historiographical works and various theories related with economic history, books as well as articles of journals. He has supplemented the findings with his own reasoning. What is probably the strength of the study is the range of economic interpretations given to the facts brought to light by historians and the urge to go beyond the realm of conventional wisdom in a logical fashion. His emphasis on the role of the humble currency media in the monetary economy of India and their eclipse in the colonial period is a special feature of this work. Anirban's book is a work of economic history written from the angle of an economist. Economists might discover in this work more of history and less of economics, while historians might see in it more of economics (and sweeping generalizations) and less of history. But a more discerning and sensible reader should be able to find something of both in this work which is well thought-out and written in a simple, lucid style. It is heartening that a reputable publisher has chosen to publish it, demonstrating the appreciation for the contents of the work rather than fame of the author.

14 September 2006

Raghabendra Chattopadhyay
Professor of Economics,
Indian Institute of Management,
Kolkata

Preface

It is perhaps needless to say that a work of this kind could not be produced without the help and cooperation of many. Professor Arun Majimdar of Viswa Bharati University first introduced me to the fascinating world of monetary history. Unfortunately, he is no more in this world to see the work in print. I should also record my deep debt of gratitude to Professor Dipak Banerjee for his constant encouragement. He is also now called to eternal rest. For library work, my biggest debt is to the courteous staff of the Centre for Studies in Social Sciences, namely Sri Kaliprasad Bose, Sri Ashutosh Chakrabarty, Sri Ramkrishna Datta, Smt Jayati Nayek, Sri Soumitra Chattopadhyay and others. Mr R.N. Vaisya, Deputy Librarian of the Central Reference Library, Delhi University and Mr H. Ratnagar, a senior employee of the periodical section of the same, cooperated very much.

For various kinds of help, I should acknowledge my debt to Professor Anup Sinha, Professor Suchibrata Sen, Professor Dhires Bhatacharya, Professor Raghabendra Chattopadhyay, Professor Kalynabrata Bhattacharya, Professor Sudip Chaudhuri, Dr Keya Dasgupta, Dr Ranjan Gupts, Dr Bhaskar Mukhopadhyay, Sri Pradosh Nath, Sri Prabir Basu, Sri Amit Ghosh, Sri Sushanta Raha, Sri Braja Kishore Datta, Sri Biplab Das and Sri Amartya Ghosh. To Vaskar Nandy and Dr Vasanti Raman, I am grateful for broadening my horizon of thought.

Some parts of the materials contained in this work were published in the form of articles in *Frontier, Bengal : Past and Present* and *Calcutta Historical Journal*. I am grateful to the editors of these journals. I owe a special debt of gratitude to Sri Kartik Chakrabarty, my computer instructor. Sri K.K. Saxena of Aakar Books has taken considerable interest in the work and provided me with warm hospitality during my stay in Delhi. A formal expression of gratitude is too inadequate for him. The usual disclaimer applies to all of the above-mentioned persons.

Preparation for this work naturally demanded frequent stays away from home, and consequent neglect of household duties. Jharna, my wife, cheerfully managed things, often taking considerable strain upon her own shoulders. Thanking her is merely presumptious, and I do not dare it.

My final thanks go to Ms Ritu Singh for the excellent editing of the manuscript.

K.C. College, Hetampur,
Birbum, West Bengal

Anirban Biswas

Abbreviations

C.S.S.S.	Centre for Studies in Social Sciences
C.U.P.	Cambridge University Press
O.U.P.	Oxford University Press
C.E.H.I.	Cambridge Economic History of India
I.E.S.H.R.	Indian Economic and Social History Review
J.E.S.H.O.	Journal of the Economic and Social History of the Orient
M.A.S.	Modern Asian Studies

Chapter One

The Rationale and Scope of the Study

Writing the monetary history of a country in transition is beset with a number of difficulties. In the Indian context, the most well-known difficulty is paucity of source material. The kind of material a research investigator requires depends, however, on the nature of the questions he or she frames. The questions framed by a student of economics are bound to be somewhat different from those posed by a historian. A researcher whose professional training is in economics might draw, quite logically, some inferences from a set of data provided by historians on the basis of his knowledge of the relationship between various macroeconomic variables. But such inferences might be unacceptable to historians who want every inference to be backed by hard empirical evidence. On the other hand, historians might be prone to take some simplified versions of some economic theory for granted, neglect their later refinements, and try to search for their appositeness in explaining some sequence of data or events, often forgetting the problems and risks associated with such endeavours. In this sense, it is a happy sign that many scholars with professional training in the tools and techniques of economic analysis have taken up economic history as a subject of study and investigation. It is perhaps not an exaggeration to suggest that their painstaking efforts have produced reasonably good results.

It is well known that money as an institution appeared somewhat later than the first acts of exchange, and as a common tangible measure of value as well as a medium of exchange. As an object, it had to be sufficiently divisible while needing at the same time some sort of guarantee regarding its worth, when presented as a common measure of value.[1] This roughly conforms to the orthodox notion of money as a commodity, because the monetary unit here has a definite intrinsic worth. Again, it may be a claim as well. A modern paper note used as money represents the debt obligation of the issuing authority, namely the state or the central bank, and this is the guarantee of its worth. Such debt obligations fall within the bounds of claim. But they cannot qualify as commodity money. A standard silver coin, say that of the Mughal period in India, had a guarantee pertaining to its intrinsic metallic content. The guarantee gave it a character that qualified it as a claim besides a commodity. And again, there might have existed some substances that functioned as money with full popular acceptance, but without any such guarantee. They were also commodity money in the sense that they were in general exchangeable with other commodities. Such exchange media were not legal tender money, but often the state allowed them to circulate. They were traded commodities and those who traded in them made profits out of their business.

With the passage of time and growth of various modern monetary and credit institutions, the definition of money has expanded, and there has emerged a number of theories on how to interpret money as a social institution and as an economic category. We may eschew a discussion of these theories at least for the time being, because their relevance to a study of monetary history is not primary or crucial. Again, notwithstanding the many modern innovations in the field of monetary exchanges and claims, early monetary media that are now seldom, if at all, used for exchange purposes even in the most backward regions of the world, retain their importance as a subject of historical study, if not as anything else.

Having said this, we have an obligation to explain what monetary history precisely means, according to our own understanding. First of all, one has to clarify whether one is attempting to write a history of the coinages or currencies in use, their areas of provenance, the names of the authorities issuing them, their contents and time periods of circulation. But monetary history is much more than that. A monetary historian need not be familiar with all the techniques employed by a trained numismatist, although he might have much to learn from the latter. The domains of numismatics and history intersect, but do not necessarily coincide. Recognizing this truth, one may attempt to study how far the degree of commerce and money use was growing and in what direction they were changing in the particular time period one is studying, and how the nature of monetary media in circulation changed along with it, and what were the social economic and political forces that propelled this change.

While undertaking such a venture, one is necessarily confronted with the important problem of analyzing the relation between commerce, the state power and the nature of currencies in circulation. The question of the state is important, because changes in the character of the polity, along with newly emerging economic interests, may give rise to new monetary movements and the emergence of new types of monetary media. There are merchants' money, both in metallic and non-metallic forms, King's or Emperor's money, and modern paper money in the shape of debt obligations of the modern state or its central bank. A monetary history might be conceived as a history of the interplay of these types of monetary media and their relations with the economy. In pre-modern economies, merchants' and king's money with guaranteed intrinsic contents were important, and so were some other monetary forms which, although having some value determined by the market forces, did not require any such guarantee.

State-sponsored commerce, and the relation between the state and merchants are important aspects of pre-modern economies, although they might not be able to explain entirely the genesis and growth of commerce and money use. It is also a lesson of economic history that although merchants often devised their own monetary media, the state effectively intervened in this process. The king or the emperor had to mint his own currencies because he could thereby easily procure the goods he required from merchants, and proclaim his own sovereignty. In the battle between merchants' money and King's money, the latter was destined to win because of the latter's larger acceptability[2]. Such a victory represents some sort of centralization, no doubt. But there is definite evidence that even when the monetary system acquired a somewhat centralized character and the currencies issued by the centralized authorities came to dominate, various types of media falling outside the pale of this centralized system circulated freely, although within local or regional limits, and they often met the much-needed demand for media of exchange in various localized circuits.

In the India case, we can see that towards 700 B.C., the rise of small states and their regular armies necessitated payments in cash, and thus began the process of rudimentary coinages[3]. But we are not sure whether currency media like *cowrie,* or monetary media issued by merchants, commonly known as *sresthis* or *seths,* were not in use then. A relatively modern example of circulation of privately-sponsored media is the notes and tokens used by the country banks during the Industrial Revolution in Britain, when the Bank of England had covered quite a few decades of its existence and a large money market had developed in London.[4] The reasons why the circulation of such media, which, although not legal tender money in the usual statist sense, nevertheless acted as money in the functional sense, need to be explored, although such reasons have their variations in time and space. It is also seen that when the changes in the nature of the polity bring about in their trail some fundamental changes in the structure of the economy, new monetary media and new types of credit and banking instruments come to dominate. Here too the needs of the state and the demands of the new commercial situation seem to dictate terms. The new institutions that apparently lay outside the domain of monetary policy, but represented in their own way the rule of the new power, reinforced this. So, in writing a history of monetary transition, the role of new institutions related with the changes in the polity and structural changes in the economy is to be investigated.

Before undertaking such an attempt as ours, some methodological points should be clarified. While it is known that exchange as an economic phenomenon predates the use of money, there is a conception following Adam Smith that exchange is a natural human propensity, like division of labour. Adam Smith, universally acknowledged as the father figure of English classical political economy, put it in the following words:

"This division of labour, from which so many advantages are derived, is not originally the effect of any human wisdom, which foresees and intends this general opulence to which it gives occasion. It is the necessary, though very slow and gradual, consequence of a certain propensity in human nature which has in view no such extensive utility, the propensity to truck, barter and exchange one thing for one another."[5]

It should be noted that Karl Marx considered this proposition a misconception and attacked it with great force. Marx was a historicist to the core and consistent with this medthodological propensity, trenchantly laid bare the ahistorical character of Smith's notion in the following words:

"To all the different varieties of values in use there correspond as many different kinds of useful labour, classified according to the order, genus, species, and variety to which they belong in the social division of labour. This division of labour is a necessary condition for the production of commodities, but it does not follow, conversely, that the production of commodities is a necessary condition for the division of labour. In the primitive Indian community there is a social division of labour, without production of commodities. Or, to take an example nearer home, in every factory the labour is divided according to a system, but this division is not brought about by the operatives mutually exchanging their individual products. Only such products can become commodities with regard to each other, as result from different kinds of labour, each kind being carried on independently and for the account of private individuals."[6]

It is very interesting that about a century later, Sir J.R. Hicks made the same point in his celebrated book *Theory of Economic History*.

"The factory, though it is producing for the market, is a non-market organization *in its internal structure*. We can get some hints, from the management structure of the ordinary factory, of what a non-market production organization necessarily as."[7] (italics original). One who has gone through Hicks's treatment of the problem cannot fail to note that Hicks developed this point independently, although he must have been aware of Marx's argument. Karl Polanyi, the celebrated American social anthroplogist, also tried to study the evolution of exchange and markets as a historical category in his famous work *The Great Transformation* as well as in his other writings on the subject. Polanyi did not explicitly consider the relation between division of labour and exchange, but attempted to show the evolution of the market as a specific stage in the growth of trade.[8] What Marx, Hicks and Polanyi seem to share in common is a historical approach to the evolution of exchange, money and market.

What we should learn from these authorities is that exchange is not a natural but a historical phenomenon, which has to be studied in its own right as a subject of history. Use of money as a universal means of exchange is certainly predated by barter of commodities, and in this sense money is also a historical category within the broader history of exchange. Although we need not label it as an eternal category, it goes without saying that there is little possibility of its abolition as a means of exchange in the foreseeable future. The very relations of production and distribution that are present almost everywhere in modern society constantly create and recreate the conditions for the use of money. Unless these relations, which are embedded in various kinds of differences and contradictions, are wiped out, use of money cannot possibly be abolished. Unsuccessful attempts at lessening or abolishing the use of money were provided by the former Soviet Union under War Communism and more recently by Pol Pot's Cambodia.

Yet one might ask with reason: how far is money a mover of historical changes? Traditionally, precious metals like gold and silver and other durable metals like copper were used as money. Obsessions with precious metals led a famous economic historian, Earl Hamilton, to attribute a major role to the import of American gold and silver in bringing about a 'price revolution' in Europe and in fostering the growth of capitalism.[9]

More curious is the fact that John Maynard Keynes, who broadened the notion about the functions of money and demolished the idea of the so-called 'money-neutrality' of variables like the level of income, employment and rate of interest, and yet rejected the purely monetary solution to the ills of capitalism, wrote: "It would be a fascinating task to rewrite Economic History .... from its remote beginnings; to conjecture whether the civilizaions of Sumeria and Egypt drew their stimulus from the gold of Arabia and the copper of Africa, which, being monetary metals, left a trail of profit behind them in the course of their distribution through the sands between the Mediterranean and the Persian Gulf, and probably farther afield; in what degree the greatness of Athens depended on the silver mines of Laurium—not because the monetary metals are more truly wealth than other things, but because by their effect on prices they supply the spur of profit; how far the dispersal by Alexander of the bank reserves of Persia, which represented the accumulated withdrawal into the treasure of successive empires during many preceding centuries, was responsible for the outburst of economic progress in the Mediterranean basin, of which Carthage attempted and Rome ultimately succeeded to reap the fruits; whether it was a coincidence that the decline and fall of Rome was contemporaneous with the most prolonged and drastic deflation ever recorded; if the long stagnation of the Middle Ages may not have been more surely and inevitably caused by Europe's meagre supply of the monetary metals than by monasticism or Gothic frenzy."[10]

In this view, expressed in a fashion that sounds almost lyrical, what is ignored is that the supply of gold, silver and copper does not automatically mean that they will circulate as money and, second, even if they do circulate as money and push up prices (the causal link between the amount of money in circulation and the price level is however not necessarily straightforward and direct), this itself need not be viewed as a prime moving factor in economic transition. A person having a nodding acquaintance with the economic history of pre-colonial India is familiar with the fact that much of the precious metals to which Earl Hamilton, who made the first authentic study of the inflow of precious metals from the New World into Europe, attributed such a big role in the rise of capitalism in the Occident, finally found its way into India and China by way of Euro-Asiatic trade and Indian merchants also acquired large amounts of wealth by means of participation in this trade in various capacities. But, curiously enough, neither India nor China moved into a capitalist phase of transition.

It is perhaps fairer to accept that the problem of transition is far more complex than can be encountered by such facile monetarism. Regarding the European transition, we can in all fairness refer to the Dobb-Sweezy debate—we should note that there were quite a few other participants in the debate—and the subsequent polemic named the Brenner Debate.[11] While the debate, particularly the latter one, has many nuances, all of which we need not go into right now, at least one point is clear: mere injection of money and trade could not bring about the dissolution of feudalism, let alone the rise of capitalism, even in Europe. Yet feudalism dissolved in Europe and capitalism rose. Neither Hamilton nor Keynes explored the subject of transition from feudalism to capitalism in any great detail, a task that later historians and economists—particularly of the Marxist variety—undertook, and both were hence apparently prone to believe in the effectiveness of gold and silver in bringing about the European transition.

The country which supposedly first experienced the 'price revolution' owing to the inflow of large amounts of American treasure, however, failed to promote capitaist development on her own soil. Studying the Spanish development of that period, one authority, Perry Anderson, was constrained to say on the effect of the influx of bullion on agriculture and manufacturing:

"But the ultimate damage caused by the colonial nexus was not limited to agriculture, the dominant branch of domestic production at the time. For the influx of bullion from the New World also produced a parasitism that increasingly sapped and halted domestic manufactures."[12]

Had the West European context been different from what it really was, no Hamilton or Keynes could have conceived of attributing such a big role to inflows of gold and silver as monetary metals in shaping the course of economic history. The outcomes of struggles involving the various social classes, coupled with technological and demographic factors, were crucial to the creation of the new context in which monetary metals and mercantile profits could play their historical roles. This has to be understood in order to grasp the idea that historical movements were not merely products of the inflow of monetary metals.

What we can learn from this debate is that while growth and extension of money use certainly indicate a genesis and proliferation of the exchange economy in a social formation, whether or not an exchange economy sets in motion a process of spiraling economic stagnation or one of economic growth is determined by its interconnection with the real variables, e.g. the nature of production relations or the nature of structuralization of generation as well as utilization of social surplus within a set of historic-institutional parameters.

Then why should one undertake to write a monetary history at all? We can suggest an answer, namely that changes in the nature of exchange media constitute one important manifestation of the general socio-economic transition. As Fernand Braudel aptly remarks on the relationship between society and money : "In fact it can come into being when men need it and can bear its cost. Its flexibility and complexity are functions of the flexibility and complexity of the economy that brings (it) into being. There will ultimately be as many types of money and monetary system as there are rhythms, systems and economic situations."[13]

One can give enough historical examples to illustrate this proposition. The changes brought about in the West European economy in the 16th-17th centuries brought about a financial revolution as well, which in turn facilitated the emergence of the Industrial Revolution by popularizing financial instruments that had not been much in use earlier.[14] Conversely, the attempted use of paper money under various regimes since the 12th century failed in China, because the nature of the economic institutions, the character of the polity and most important, the existing level of confidence or loyalty of the money-using people on the issuing authorities and the level of integration of the economy did not support it, and China had, after a number of experiments with the paper currency, eventually to switch to a silver standard.[15] In India, the changes introduced by the colonizing British rulers were of far-reaching consequence for the economy and there took place, amidst new conflicts and tensions, important changes in the sphere of money and banking. But there is no evidence of circulation of paper money in the precolonial period. Of course, *hundis*, i.e., bills of exchange and promissory notes, circulated on a limited scale, but they were not paper currency in the sense of tokens of debt-obligations of the state. Monetary history is, in this sense, a reflection of real history, whether the former has any serious causal significance in shaping the latter.

Some general sequences in the evolution in the nature of monetary media are, however, observable. The category called 'money' can, in one sense, be divided into two broad types, commodity money and token money. Examples of the former are metallic currencies. They are commodities in the sense that they have both use value and exchange value. Token currencies, e.g., modern paper currencies issued by the state or the central bank, on the other hand, have exchange value, but no use value. Token money, in the course of time, came to dominate and eventually replace commodity money. This happened in Europe, this happened in India, this happened in China (long after the failure of the early experiments, however) and so on and so forth. But in every case there were definite historical phases in which such replacements were feasible. The degree of such feasibility depended on the acceptability of the sovereignty of the issuing authorities by the public at large, and second, by the capability of the authorities to issue them in enough quantities. The old forms of commodity money, even when issued by the state, depended for their worth on their intrinsic contents. The function of the state was to provide a guarantee about these contents. And it was because these contents had alternative uses that they qualified as commodity money. In the Indian contxt, it might be argued that the introduction and development of the use of paper money and

European-style banking was definitely a byproduct of the colonial hegemony over the monetary sphere. In the pre-colonial period, there were currencies in circulation not devised by the state or by big merchant-bankers. Those currencies were eclipsed in the colonial period in consequence of the economic and political changes that the colonizing rulers brought in. Among these changes three can be specially noted. One was the institution of Permanent Settlement of land revenue, the second was the attempt at the unification of currency in a situation of shortage of older currency media, coupled with introduction of European-style banking, and the third was the frantic bid to control the market places. During the first a few decades of colonial rule, these endeavours were undertaken in a situation of general price rise, which was largely the outcome of the commercial policy of the new rulers.

The objective set by this study does not promise exploration of all the ramifications of the difference between India's pre-colonial monetary order and the monetary order imposed on the Indian subcontinent by the colonizing rulers. In fact, there is an excellent and voluminous work on the colonial monetary order by an eminent economist of our time.[16] Also, we have a good number of investigative research articles and some good books on various aspects of the commerce and monetary order of pre-colonial India. But there are few studies in which the vital aspects of the transition from the pre-colonial to the colonial monetary order have been investigated in a comprehensive manner and the qualitative nature of the changes properly noted. Understanding these vital aspects, and linking them with the changes brought about by the colonial rule are important and we have made a humble attempt to set up these links, at least partially.

Before entering into the subject of transition, we have tried to present a brief survey of the monetary order of Mughal India, and contemporary Deccan and south India. One of our points of emphasis is the importance of the non-imperial and non-royal currency media, the media that lent the monetary system a pluralistic and somewhat decentralized character.

At this juncture, we may point out that in so far as historicotheoretical writings on monetary media are concerned, the overwhelming burden of emphasis so far is on precious metals. This is observable in both Adam Smith and Karl Marx. This can be said about Keynes as well, as our citation, made a little earlier, shows. About the relatively recent authorities too, it can be said that the emphasis is regrettably on money in the form of precious metals. This concentration is demonstrated in Pierre Vilar's celebrated book, *A History of Gold and Money* as well as in a recent scholarly work, *A History of Money*, written by John Chown.

While the former contains one or two references to India, and the existence of fiduciary money along with 'strong' currencies, the latter concentrates exclusively on money in the European perspective. In respect of Indian historical scholarship too, it is noticeable that the humble currency media constitute a neglected, although worthwhile, subject of study. One can have a look at the writings of the so-called Aligarh school of historians, whose scholarship is otherwise impeccable and exemplary in many cases, in order to understand this unfortunate neglect.

So, in order to have a proper comprehension of the subject, one has to comprehend the role these media had in the monetary system of pre-colonial India and the reasons why they declined under the new dispensation brought about by the British. Of course, other changes in the monetary sphere have to be noted, but the important task is to understand how all the changes were linked with the transformations in the economy and polity that the colonial rule had brought in. It should be noted that the course of transition had significant regional variations, and a selective approach is necessary if the phenomenon has to be captured within the limited space of a short monograph like this.

We have taken up Bengal as a case study of the transition from the pre-colonial commercial-cum-monetary order to the colonial one, and preambled it with our discussion on the nature of use of money in Mughal India and contemporary South and the Deccan. Generally our temporal focus is on the 17th-18th centuries, as the reader will be able to observe. The choice of Bengal as the focal point of study is not an arbitrary one, nor is the product of some nationalistic enthusiasm on the part of the author, but is dictated by some definite considerations. The selection of Bengal is not dictated by the fact of its being the first region to enter the colonial political nexus, but also by some other reasons, the reasons that prompted the European companies and other Asian and European merchants to brave the rough journeys to Bengal's dominant centre of water-borne trade at Hooghly.

The first and foremost reason is that Bengal was the producer of much lucrative merchandise at such low costs that currencies produced by imperial mints did not suffice for her monetary transactions, and various types of silver coins had to be supplemented by non-metallic *cowrie* currencies particularly in low-priced exchanges. We should add here that it was not the widspread circulation of the *cowrie* currency in rural *haats* and semi-urban *bazaars* and *ganjs*—markets that served as centres of sale of goods—but the cheapness (one of the reasons underlying the widespread use of the low value, non-imperial *cowrie* currency) and variety of Bengal's merchandise that attracted the East India Companies and various Asian merchants to this region.

The second reason was that Bengal in the pre-colonial period seemingly remained remarkably free from any inflationary trend, which supposedly affected other regions of Mughal India. Apart from the studies based on Company records and the persuasive arguments that these studies have made on this subject, it may be noted that all through the pre-colonial period, the *cowrie* currency, several units of which were required to form a viable unit of exchange, dominated small transactions, which clearly would not have been possible in a situation of continuing price rise. The *cowrie* currency was considered synonymous with money itself in Bengal; hence its disappearance from circulation certainly forms an important aspect of monetary transition in this region in the colonial period. But this aspect has not possibly received the attention it deserves.

The historical fact of Bengal falling under colonial subjugation before other regions is also important, however. It is important because the monetary experiments of the colonial state were launched first in this region and the impact on the monetary shpere was profound and far-reaching. This was a period of chronic disequilibria produced, ironically, by the attempt of the colonial state to end a situation that the colonizers themselves considered less than orderly. However, some sort of stability and order was eventually brought about, but it took a long time to come and it could not be achieved without the promulgation and implementation of other measures that supplemented these experimants. While it is true that the discorder and stringency, which made it imperative for the Company to undertake these experiments, were themselves products of its policy of conquest and extraction, the success of these experiments depended crucially on the creation of new institutions, which did not always have direct monetary appearance, but which helped in preparing the colonial terrain for gradually consolidating the hegemony of the colonizing state. This hegemony was important in the transition to a new monetary order, but it was not achievable by just creating new financial institutions and introducing new rupees and other coins. Hence, it needs to be pondered how far these financial and non-financial institutions taken together might have accelerated the establishment of the colonial hegemony in the monetary sphere. The process of colonization led to the eclipse, not only of old monetary media, but of old money-dealing classes as well, and the role of those that newly emerged as collaborators of the new regime was drastically different owing to the differences in historical context. Keeping in mind the importance of outlining the contextuall underpinning, we have tried to discuss at some length all these points, in the hope that more scholarly persons would throw greater light on them in the future.

NOTES AND REFERENCES

1. For a lucid and standard treatment of the origin of money from the angle of an economist, one can still read Adam Smith's *An Inquiry into the Nature and Causes of the Wealth of Nations*. Pelican, 1974, Chs. IV & V : 126–150.

2. J.R. Hicks caught this point well enough when he wrote, "When Croesus, King of Lydia, minted coins, he .... was giving the money a guarantee, which made it more acceptable. There was an advantage to him in doing this, since he could then more easily use it to get the goods he required, or might require, from the merchants who were his neighbours. It may indeed have been the merchants who, in the first instance, insisted upon some guarantee.... A merchant's stamp might be accepted in Miletus, where he was known; but it would be much less acceptable in the hinterland, in Lydia. The King's stamp would be acceptable in his kingdom, and in the trading city". Hicks, *Theory of Economic History*, Oxford: Clarendon Press, 1969, 66–67.
3. Bhattacharya, Sukumari. *In Those Days: Essays Vedic—Epic and Classical.* Kolkata: Camp, 2001, p. 65.
4. The most authentic study of this subject is L.S. Pressnell's *Country Banking in the Industrial Revolution*. Oxford : Clarendon Press, 1956.
5. Smith, Adam. *The Wealth of Nations.* Vol. 1, Pelican, 1974, p. 15.
6. Marx, Karl. *Das Kapital*, Vol. 1. Moscow: Progressive Publishers, 1986, p. 49.
7. Hicks, op. cit., p. 10.
8. For example, vide Polanyi : The Economy as Instituted Process. In *Trade and Markets in the Early Empires*. Eds. Polanyi, Arsenberg and Pearson. The Free Press, Illinois and the Falcom's Wing Press, 1957, 243–270, "Trade as well as some money was, are as old as mankind; while markets, although meetings of an economic character may have existed as early as Neolithic, did not gain importance until comparatively late in history", Ibid, p. 256.
9. Hamilton, Earl. *American Treasure and the Price Revolution in Spain*, 1501–1650. Massachusets: Cambridge, 1936.
10. Keynes, J.M. *A Treatise on Money*. London: Macmillan. 150–151.
11. Vide the Dobb-Sweezy Debate is to be found, along with other contributions to the subject. In *The Transition from Feudalism to Capitalism*. Ed. Rodney Hilton. Verso, 1976 South Asian edition. Delhi: Aakar Books, 2006. The subsequent polemic is to be found in *The Brenner Debate : Agraian Class Structure and Economic Development in Pre-Industrial Europe*. Eds. T.H. Ashton and C.H.E. Philipin. Delhi : Foundation Books, 2005.
12. Anderson, Perry. *The Lineages of Absolutist State*, N.L.B., 1974: 72–73.

13. Braudel, Fernand. *Capitalism and Material Life.* Glasgow: Fontana/Collins, 1974 : 328.
14. Parker, Geoffrey. The Emergence of Modern Finance in Europe 1500–1730. In *The Fontana Economic History of Europe : The Sixteenth and Seventeenth Centuries.* Ed. C.M. Cipolla. Glasgow: Collins/Fontana, 1974, passim.
15. For a brief but elegant discussion, Zurndoffer Harriet T. "Another look at China, Money, Silver and the Seventeenth Century Crisis." *JESHO* 42, no. 3 (1999) : 396–411.
16. Bagchi, Amiya Kumar. *The Evolution of the State Bank of India.* O.U.P., 1986.
17. Vilar, Pierre. *A History of Gold and Money.* N.L.B, 1976. John Chown. *A History of Money from A.D. 800,* London and New York: Routledge, 1996.

Chapter Two

The Monetary System, Use of Money and Commerce in Mughal India

A student of the economic history of pre-colonial India must revel in the fact that a considerable body of works has been published on various aspects of the subjects, ranging from revenue system, production and technology to commerce and money use. There are regional studies as well as attempts at broader generalizations. It should be noted that much of the literature has referred to Mughal India, the Mughal period and the state and economy under the Mughals, directly and indirectly. Of course, what is called Mughal India was in a state of continuous expansion and contraction, and there were some regions that never fell within the Mughal domain. Yet the emphasis has some justifiction at least. First of all, the Mughal empire was stretched over a considerable part of the territory of pre-colonial India for about two centuries, and more important, the Mughals tried to set up a centralized system of administration on the basis of a coherent mode of revenue assessment and collection, and a uniform and organized monetary order. As Tapan Raychaudhuri, in a review article published four decades ago on the dynamics of the agrarian economy of Mughal India, put it succinctly, "The transition from a decentralized revenue administration with practically hereditary *jagirdars*, collection in kind and relatively unobtrusive central administration to the Mughal system of revenue demand in cash, transferable *jagirs* and the increasing financial needs of a powerful, expanding and centralized empire is crucial in this context."[1] It goes without saying that such centralization required the circulation of some sort of uniform King's money, or a hierarchy of uniform currencies. So, the Mughals had to devise a monetary order that could proclaim their sovereignty, and at the same time facilitated the extraction of economic surplus by them from producers and traders and to distribute this surplus among the various dependent classes, besides reproducing themselves. It is easily inferable that owing to the diversity between production and consumption needs as between localities, areas and regions, this distribution of surplus was impossible without a network of trade and commerce and movement of cash, either physically or through bills, throughout the empire in order to be effective, and this required the establishment of a monetary order acceptable to the parties involved in this movement. So, studying the Mughal monetary economy must involve a discussion of the monetary media that evolved under Mughal rule, as well as the nature of the trade and commerce that grew in the Mughal period.

Studying the monetary order that functioned in the Mughal empire and the nature of commerce that developed in Mughal India does not however dispense with the need to investigate the pattern of money use and the nature and types of currencies in circulation in non-Mughal arreas, nor does it mean that the entire pattern of money use even in the Mughal areas can be adequately studied within the framework of the monetary system that the Mughal imperial rulers themselves devised. A proper understanding of the monetary economy of pre-colonial India requires that the similarities and differences between the Mughal and non-Mughal areas be properly comprehended, and regional variations properly noted. Even within the Empire, there were inevitably considerable regional variations, which should be taken account of as far as possible. In this chapter, we wish to place our understanding of the monetary economy of Mughal India, purporting to take up the second issue in the next one. We have, however, to keep in mind that there were considerable intercourses between the Mughal and non-Mughal regions by way of trade and transfer of funds. This knowledge should help us in liberating ourselves from what is sometimes called Mughal-centrism, a standing reproach against some historians. A careful look at regional variations would reveal that there were many elements in the Mughal economy that were not characteristically 'Mughal'.

THE SYSTEM OF TRIMETALLISM

There is now virtually a universal agreement among historians that the prosperity and power of the Mughals depended on the agricultural wealth of the empire and that they laid a great deal of emphasis on the acquistion of rent in money form (increasing use of the *zabt* system)[2]. With the expansion of the Empire, mints were set up in every provincial capital and important trading centres. The Mughals also underlook the minting of coins in their names as a symbol of authority. This is proved by the fact that although foreign coins such as *reals* and *larins* were imported into Mughal India, they had to be recoined into Mughal silver currencies before entering the arena of circulation.[3] *Larins* served as units of account or means of payment in some coastal areas, Mughal and non-Mughal, but at least as far as Mughal India was concerned, they were not allowed to be used for transactions in the interior. Of course, uniformity of coinage was a convenient method of distribution of surplus over the empire when use of coined money had become the vougue. Possibly in view of this consideration, and also with the purpose of proclaiming the sovereignty of the state, the Mughals tried to impse their monetary writ over the areas that came under their control in course of the process of expansion of the empire.[5]

The growth of the *mansabdari* system, i.e., the system of revenue assignments to imperial officers commanding troops for their own salaries as well as well as for payments to soldiers, promoted the use of money as a fiscal device. There is disagreement over the relative importance of bankers in the Mughal period, but it is accepted that over time, there was a gradual development of the credit system and transfer of funds by means of bills of exchange, which only indicates a growth of monetisation. The revenue assessments made in the celebrated *Ain-i-Akbari* also are shown in general in terms of the copper *dam*, the copper currency of the Mughals.

From the general information provided by Irfan Habib and other Aligarh historians, it is known that the Mughal monetary order was a hierarchy of three metallic coins, (i) gold *muhr*, (ii) silver *rupayaa* or rupee, and (iii) the copper *dam*. It is also known that it was a system of free minting, implying that anybody could take the metal to the mint and have it coined after paying the necessary mint charges.[6] It means that the output of currency was demand-determined subject, however, to the constraint of the number and capacity of mints. It is clear that under such a system, no legally fixed ratio of the three coins could last, hence three sub-systems of prices and money wages could operate. The coins had little alloy content and the norms of standardization were scrupulously followed. So, the relative prices of the three coins varied according to the vicissitudes in the prices of gold, silver and copper. There was no uniform accounting money, and the role of the state was to guarantee the intrinsic content of the minted coins. In this sense, the Mughal legal tender money was commodity money *par excellence*. From the research on the coinage system of Mughal India, it is also known that there was a reduction in mint seigniorage over time,[7] showing that the monetary policy of the Mughals was increasingly favourable to the promotion of trade. The expansion of the empire, and the Mughals' attempt to introduce everywhere a uniform currency system through receipt of revenues in standard imperial coins also increased the demand for these coins.

It is easily understandable that the relative prices of the three metals and hence the relative roles of the three currencies in the monetary system could not remain static over time, and were liable to vary according to the vicissitudes of demand and supply. The fluctuations in the relative supplies of gold, silver and copper in the Indian subcontinent in the 17th century have been assiduously discussed by historians. It should be mentioned at the outset that the amount of extraction of silver and gold was very little in the Mughal empire, and the amount of indigenous copper production was far too short of demand. Hence, the imperial monetary system was very much dependent on imports of these metals. Another source was definitely successive conquests, extraction of tributes from the vanquished and plunder. But that could by no means be the major source of metallic money of an empire that ruled over a vast territory for more than a century at least, and tried to make it as stable as possible. With the expansion and consolidation of the empire, there was a steady decline of such sources.

It is well known that the discovery of silver mines in the New World in the 16th century was followed by the influx of huge amounts of silver into Europe. A considerable part of this silver reached India and China through the channels of Euro-Asiatic trade, after a certain time lag. The Portuguese dominated the Indo-European trade in the 16th century, but thereafter the Dutch, French and English East India Companies entered the scene in a big way. It should be noted that there was a large European demand for Indian goods, especially cotton textiles, in the 17th-18th centuries. These goods were purchased largely, although not entirely, with the help of the gold and silver of the Americas. Besides, European Companies were involved in Asian trade and needed Indian goods for sale in Asian markets.

On the impact of this silver inflow on the Mughal economy, there has been much discussion. Heavy silver coins began to be struck at the mints of Sher Shah, who briefly interrupted Mughal rule in 1540. But it is difficult to relate this phenomenon with the import of American silver into Europe and the redirection of a considerable part of it to India.[8] During the first half of the administration of Akbar (1556-1605) a process of replacement of copper by silver had begun, although silver was not yet the dominant currency metal in the empire'[9]. It may be noted that the six decades from around the 1540s were the period when there was an inundation of silver in Europe.[10] There is no doubt that much of this silver reached the Indian subcontinent after certain time lags by way of Indo-European trade, although there were short-term fluctuations in this inflow.

The Aligarh view of the subject can be summarized into two main conclusions: one, since the closing years of the 16th century, the position of copper as the dominant currency metal began to decline and it was replaced by silver, and two, the money supply in the empire grew largely, resulting in an inflation (termed 'price revolution' by Habib, probably following the use of the same by Earl Hamilton in the context of Spain)[12]. It might be mentioned in passing that a similar proposition was put forward in the context of Ming China by William S. Atwell and others.[12] The Aligarh view generated some debate and we wish to survey it briefly in the hope that it might provide us with some more insights into the pattern of money use in circulation.

On the impact of the inflow of silver, some points that have emerged from the studies on the subject may be noted. The last quarter of the sixteenth century witnessed massive imports of silver into Mughal India via the channels of European trade. But at least till 1610-15, there was no discernible upward trend in the price of copper in term of silver.[13] This trend appeared thereafter, giving rise to the ascendancy of silver as the principal monetary metal.

There is virtually no disagreement that the rupee, along with its fractional piece, *anna,* came to be the dominant coin in the first half of the 17th century, and that the Mughals tried to enforce their monetary system throughout the empire including the conquered territories. As J.F. Richards suggested, "The Mughal coinage system, with its uniform imperial standards of weights and measures, was imposed throughout the subcontinent over dozens of local monetary systems. The finance ministry's unyielding requirement that all tribute and tax be paid in imperial coin was the effective impulse for diffusion of the rupee. The imperial system of so-called free minting by individuals and forced use of rupees for taxes and official disbursement purposes provided a mechanism for converting the vast sums of foregn bullion and specie which annually poured into Indian ports."[14] But what is not so agreeable is that these sums of bullion and specie, after being coined into Mughal currencies and entering into circulation, gave birth to a general inflation or 'price revolution.'

It is worth noting that even in the European context, the notion of a one-to-one correspondence between the inflow of precious metals and the 'price revolution' has been challenged forcefully by recent historical research, and much inter-temporal incongruity between the 'price revolution' and inflow of American silver has been discovered. The 'price revolution' is found to have begun earlier then the inflow of American silver.[15]

The hypothesis of inflation or 'price revolution' in the context of Mughal India was first systematically put forward in a paper by Aziza Hasan in 1969. Aziza Hasan, on the basis of the museum catalogues, tried to estimate the relative variations of the silver currency output of the empire and to correlate it with the evidence on prices in Delhi and Agra, and with the data on the influx of New World silver into Europe. Shireen Moosvi, in her book on the Mughal empire, attempted to fortify Hasan's conclusions, but she made her estimates of the currency output by using the treasure troves of Uttar Pradesh.[16] Habib's principal contribution to the subject was to find out, from different records, the trend in *rupayaa* prices of the *dam* and the *muhr*. According to Habib's findings, the fall in the relative prices of silver was less fully reflected in gold prices than in copper prices.[17] It should be noted that in a paper published about the same time, Shireen Moosvi provided a somewhat well-argued explanation for this phenomenon. In this paper, Moosvi largely departed from her earlier view on inflation and argued, "The only series, though broken and inadequate, are those of gold and copper prices in terms of silver. We know something about the supply of both gold and copper; and we can, therefore, consider their price movements as reflective of the general purchasing power of the rupee, subject to such deviations as must have taken place by changes in the demand and supply position of the other two metals." She wisely distinguished between the general price level of commodities and copper prices and concluded, ".... if we forget for the moment our estimates of silver stock, our information about copper alone should have suggested that the general price level could not have doubled between 1615 and 1705, and since this is the scale of increase in price of copper, and that was a commodity which was exceptionally scarce. On the other hand, gold (33%) is more likely to give a true reflection of rise of the general price level since the conditions of its demand remained about the same and its supply increased modestly."[19] In a more recent paper, Moosvi suggests a low rate of inflation, 0.83 per cent per annum for goods.[20] It appears that using copper prices as a proxy for goods prices have led to some erroneous conclusions about the magnitude of inflation in Mughal India. It may be mentioned in passing that even the most virulent critic of the thesis of price revolution, namely Sanjay Subrahmanyam, has not opposed the findings on the appreciation of copper prices.

The reasons for the scarcity of copper are fairly easy to comprehend. There was a fall in copper production in Europe in the 16th century and a consequent decline in lagging copper imports into India.[21] Imports of Japanese copper by the Dutch East India Company were a phenomenon that began around the 1650s. Besides, a point mentioned by Habib and elaborated by Moosvi should be noted. Copper was a substitute for both iron and silver, while gold was a substitute only for silver. Copper was needed for the production of armaments, and since the internecine war for accession to the throne in 1658-59, large amounts of copper went into this activity, instead of being coined to the used as money[22]. The notion of a general decline in the production of copper coins in Mughal India is also supported by John S. Deyell's findings.[23]

Considering this point, it should be accepted, notwithstanding Fank Perlin's unsubstantiated contention that copper returned to the Mughal mint in a major way during the closing decades of the 17th century,[24] that the copper coinage of the Mughal empire went into a general decline after the ascendancy of silver as the dominant currency metal. Perlin's contention might well have a good deal of validity for the western Deccan in view of his own serious research work on the nature and extent of monetary circulation in that region, but it is very difficult to accept his proposition in the context of north India.

En passant, it may be mentioned that in Ming China too there was a decline in the silver-gold price ratio, and a much larger fall in the silver-copper price ratio. In China, the amount of gold entering into circulation was small, and likewise, gold *muhrs* in India were used only for high-value trade and hoarding. This could not be otherwise, because as per findings, the price of gold relative to silver was higher in India than in China till the mid-17th century.[25] Of course, the gold-silver price ration had fluctuations and sometimes went down discernibly, e.g. in the last quarter of the 17th century, leading to the surmise that gold coins entered into circulation on a wider scale,[26] but this does not invalidate the conclusion of the limited nature of its use in monetary exchanges.

The original as well as revised views of the Aligarh historians are, however, problematic in some other respects. despite Shireen Moosvi's sensible correction. Shireen Moosvi came to the conclusion that between 1595 and 1705, the price level increased by about 27%, considering the change in the G.N.P. Taking into account the modest rise (33%) in the supply of gold and the relatively unchanged condition of its demand, she drew the inference that the general price level, i.e., the purchasing power of the rupee, was more truly reflected in this supply rather than in that of silver.[27] But whatever the corrections in the method of estimation of silver output, trying to relate the silver currency output with the change in the general price level in a direct manner is fraught with many difficulties. Another problem is to relate the currency output with the influx of silver from Europe, because there are reasons to believe that there were considerable imports of Japanese silver by the Dutch East India Company into India in the 17th century, particularly during the three decades from 1640.[28]

Besides, there are other inadeqacies of the Aligarh approach. First of all, the Aligarh historians have largely ignored regional differences in respect of price movements. In the case of Bengal, arguably the most commercially ebullient region of the empire, there are strong reasons to belive that there was no significant price movement in the 17th-18th centuries before the decisive colonial victory in 1757. Combining the highly persuasive arguments of two distinguished students of the economic history of pre-colonial India, namely Sushil Chaudhuri and Om Prakash, such a picture seems to emerge.[29] Apart from the findings of these scholars, there is the incontestable historical fact that Bengal continued to use an extremely low-priced non-minted currency medium, *cowrie*, in its small exchanges in an undiminishaed fashion, which would not have been possible in the face of sustained price rise over a long period. The regional differences in respect of price movement have not unfortunately engaged the attention of Aligarh scholars, and they have in general eschewed the subject.

The theoretical problems associated with the Aligarh approach may also be noted. Both Habib and Moosvi have suggested a fall in the rate of interest, and Moosvi has collected a good deal of information on this subject, constantly emphasizing this phenomenon.[30] An unavoidable theoretical necessity is to examine whether a fall in the rate of interest increases the demand for money by lowering the velocity of circulation of money. In that event, the case of inflation is seriously weakened. It is interesting that Habib, while conceding the possibility of a fall in the rate of interest, argues that the veolcity of circulation might have risen, forgetting that the two phenomena do not easily go together.[31] It should be understood that a fall in the nominal rate of interest, by reducing the opportunity cost of holding money as inventory, reduces its velocity of circulation and thereby increases the transactions demand for money at the same level of real income and prices. (This understanding need not take us to the Keynesian notion of liquidity preference).[32] It is notable that not only Habib, but even Braudel and Spooner in their authentic survey on the price movement in Europe have not touched on this point.[33] It might be suggested that while the development of a market in *hundis* (bills of exchange) and the growing use of these papers for spatial transfer of money led to an increase in the velocity of circulation, the fall in the rate of interest had a depressing effect on it, so that the final impact on the demand for money and hence on the nominal price level could be very much indeterminate. Now, there is another problem, i.e. that of reconciling the increase in the price level with the fall in the rate of interest. The rise in the price level, by raising the transactions demand for money, should exercise an upward raising influence on the nominal rate of interest, not depress it, if the rise in the price level is the direct outcome of increased money supply. If the rise of money supply far outweighs the change in the transactions demand and the rise in the price level, then, however, the rate of interest might eventually fall. Whether such a phenomenon occurred in Mughal India, at least in its core regions, is not yet known with any degree of certainty.

It is noteworthy that the entire discussion on the price revolution has been conducted in terms of urban prices. Data on rural prices are much more difficult to obtain, but this leaves a big gap in the studies that have been made. If we do not assume that there was a synchronization between the markets where goods are first transacted and those where they are puchased for final consumption, we have to recognize the problem. Within the narrow spatial range of the study, one may however, conceive of regional differences in the rates of growth of effective demand as an explanation of price differentials. From whatever evidence we do have at out disposal, it seems that the population of the cities like Agra and Surat rose substantially in the 17th century.[34] Even if it is conceded that the so-called 'price revolution' took place in these cities, but not in Bengal's towns, such as Hooghly and Murshidabad owing to a relatively slow growth of urban effective demand, the price differential remains unexplained, because the relative lack of domestic urban demand was in all probability adequately compensated by the external demand for Bengal's goods, a subject which we shall have occasions to dwell on later.

From the debate on the inflation or 'price revolution', however, two points seem to have emerged clearly. First of all, the huge influx of silver bullion went primarily into circulation, not into hoarding. This leads to the conclusion that there was a demand for these bullions in the Indian economy, just as there was a flourishing demand for Indian manufactures in European markets. Hence the imported silver (or for that matter, gold, copper, etc.) should be taken not just as a means of payment or balancing items on the part of Europeans; they should be treated as commodities, rather than as means of payment. Had there been no demand for these commodities in the Indian subcontinent, they would not have been received in exchange of

Indian manufactures, and this demand was less to satisfy any oriental penchant for ornaments than to meet the growing transactions demand for money. It is important to remember that although precious metals were exported from India particularly for the import of things like good quality horses,[35] unlike today's dollar currencies so coveted by the ruling governments and the economic elite of most of the developing countries, they were generally received not in order to make international payments, but for internal purposes like coining, and to some extent hoarding. Besides, it should be kept in mind that gold, silver and copper and also *cowrie* (about the alternative uses of *cowrie* we shall comment later) had definite alternative uses, which qualified them as commodities. The second point, noted by both Habib and Moosvi, is that the copper coin was scarce even when the imports of copper picked up in the closing decades of the 17th century. In this case, the rise in the price of copper must have been higher not in terms of the silver rupee, but in respect of goods as well. The copper coin having been scarce, many smaller transactions were too low-priced even for a copper *dam*. In this case, the alternative is to revert to some sort of barter exchange, or to use some other currency media that fetched lower market prices than a single unit of copper *dam*. Once this point is accepted, we have to look beyond the imperial monetary system of trimetallism in order to comprehend the pattern of money use in Mughal India itself. This we propose to discuss later in this chapter. The thrust of our argument is that we should accord proper places to non-Mughal humbler and cruder currency media in order to understand the nature and scale of monetization in Mughal India.

It may be mentioned that the whole argument on the thesis of the 'price revolution' has been constructed on the basis of urban prices, and although agricultural commodities have been considered, their prices in urban centres have been taken into account. These commodities enter the marketing nexus only through rural sites of exchange, and without a consideration of the prices prevailing there, it is doubtful whether any thesis or hypothesis of the occurrence of inflation or 'price revolution' can be constructed at all.

MARKETS IN THE MUGHAL EMPIRE

In order to have a fuller understanding of the pattern of use of money in Mughal India, we can reasonably attempt an examination of the nature of market formations at various levels in the Mughal empire. The study of markets, especially rural markets, seems to be a relatively unexplored area of the historiography of pre-colonial India as a whole. It should be pointed out at the outset that with the growth of the process of centralization of the bureaucracy and the army along with the process of imperial expansion, the need for money on the part of the Mughal establishment grew and there was a concurrent spread of spatial transfer of goods and money. Monetization promotes the growth of markets. One of the points needing examination is whether the markets that existed in the Mughal empire, particularly in the countryside, functioned simply as a part of the state-driven commercial network, i.e. in order to provide a space to the peasants and artisans for collection of money for revenue payment in exchange of their produce and to allow merchants to transfer the real counterpart of this surplus to towns so as to meet the consumption needs of the revenue-appropriating classes. From this view, direct producers, i.e. peasants and artisans had no independent monetized exchanges among themselves, and the real surplus was bought by merchants and taken to towns. The proceeds of this sale were more or less exhausted by the needs of tributary revenue payment. This is a view dominantly put forward by the foremost scholar on the Mughal economy, namely Professor Irfan Habib. In his book *The Agrarian System of Mughal India*, Habib put forward the notion of a close correspondence between surplus extraction and marketing in villages. Later, in 1969, he argued this point in stronger terms and went on to conclude".... Here it must be considered whether the entire commercial structure of the Mughal Indian economy was not largely parasitical, depending upon a system of direct agrarian exploitation by a small ruling class. It is not to be forgotten that practically no rural market existed for urban crafts; rural monetization was thus entirely the result of the need to transfer surplus agricultural produce to the towns."[36] The same idea has been explicitly suggested by Blake and implicitly assumed by J.F. Richards.[37] Tapan Raychaudhuri's position in this regard is somewhat self-contradictory. In his article referred to at the beginning of the chapter, he suggested that "the primary producer was not concerned with merely as a form of economic activity required to secure the wherewithal for the payment of revenue; the process of production itself had become partly dependent on exchange operations." In the same article, however, he went on to comment that, "...for all practival purposes, the process of monetization stopped at the border of village India."[38] Subsequently, he put forward a more cautious opinion and said, "The collection of revenue in cash generated a pressure to sell; the towns, providing the necessary demand, were dependent on the villages for the supply of not only the primary products but most of the manufactured goods they consumed."[39] The 'pressure to sell' obviously implies that that there was another class of surplus appropriators, namely the merchants, which village producers had to deal with, and in this bargain, producers were likely to lose. Now the question is how these merchants should be categorized, and how the structure of mercantile operations be described. A related question is whether there was any significant scale of money use in excess of the needs of revenue payment.

At the outset, it should be made clear that there is no point in denying the importance of revenue payment as at least one explanatory variable in determining the scale of monetization. The 'pressure to sell' was obviously there because the state was overwhelmingly dependent on surplus extraction from agriculture for its maintenance and reproduction. The point is whether use of money overstepped the limits imposed by this pressure and penetrated the subsistence-oriented economy of the village peasant and artisan. In other words, the question is whether the imperatives of revenue payment constituted the only explanatory variable for determining the pace of rural monetization.

We here refer to an important and pioneering article, first published in 1966, by B.R. Grover, in which he tried to analyze the structure of the commercial economy of the rural society of north India during the 17th and 18th centuries. He highlighted the importance of local *mandis* (wholesale markets) in which groups of adjacent villages sold and purchased agricultural and industrial products. Grover also pointed out the existence of weekly or fortnightly local *mandis* "where goods were purchased or bartered by artisans". Grover also noted that "certain villages were known for religious or cultural fairs which equally served the purpose of the local markets."[40] Grover's article was a pioneering one in drawing attention to the interdependence among villages and their common use of rural markets for inter-village exchanges. A relatively recent study made by Sudipta Sen has shown with enough evidence that local chieftains in north India and Bengal used to set up markets and fairs in their areas for the twin purpose of exercise of authority and enhancement of income.[41] Tapan Raychaudhuri, in his survey of inland trade in Mughal India, pointed out that in Bengal, the establishment of *haats* (market places for periodic exchanges, held usually once or twice a week—equivalent with what Grover called local *mandis*) was the tradition of every good *zamindar*.[42] Such opinions and observations do not easily fit into a model of rural monetization and market formation driven solely by the imperatives of revenue payment. In the case of Bangal, it may be noted that *zamindars* enjoyed a considerable measure of autonomy in relation to supra-village authorities. In other places too, it is doubtful to conceive of *zamindars* as simple subordinates, acting always in order to facilitate the mode of revenue collection by the supra-village authorities and having no other consideration in the setting up of markets.

Apart from the question of local authority, the issue can be approached form another angle, namely that of economic specialization. According to Raychaudhuri himself, "It is equally certain that virtually everyone was involved in exchange as producer or consumer, usually both."[43] The implicit suggestion is that involvement in exchanges transcended the need for revenue payment. This view is strengthened when account is taken of the fact that production of cash crops like cotton and indigo was a reality in Mughal India and that the cotton grown in one place traveled via a network of borizontal and vertical exchanges, over long distances to be used by rural artisans of other places. Raychaudhuri has noted that the increasing use of the *zabt* system encouraged the production of cash crops and extension of cultivation, which was not at all infeasible in view of a favourable land-man ratio.[44] In another place, he is seen to observe, "By the mid-eighteenth century, development of market forces had made deep inroads into the subsistence character of Indian agriculture, though the producer continued to meet all his requirements of food out of his own produce.... Agriculture and horticulture in India were thus receptive to new items and responsive to market demand."[45] Receptivity to market forces implies some sort of specialization, and extension in the production of cash crops. It is unlikely that peasants specializing in the production of cash crops like indigo would barter them for collecting their necessities like food grains and cloth. Of course, it is quite possible that individual peasants conbined production of foodgrains with that of cash crops on their respective plots of land, but increse in the degree of specialization and growing penetration of market forces imply the trend towards the use of money in excess of the needs of revenue payment. So, it can be argued that although revenue payment was one of the propelling factors of rural monetization, one should be chary of emphasizing a one-to-one correspondence between the two. So, the following remark made by a young and competent researcher seems pertinent enough. "It appears that in the sixteenth and the seventeenth centuries the size of the product sold beyond the village for money increased not only under fiscal pressure but also out of the needs of the rural communities to transact the markets of the *qasbas* and towns to sell its surplus product for profit as well as obtain commodities for consumption. The specialization which grew in the rural hinterland in response to export demand and the internal demand for food-and-craft products indicated greater orientation of the village and intermediate economies towards monetized exchanges than has been acknowledged so far."[46]

It is hence not unreasonable to suppose that rural markets

in Mughal India grew up as parts of the village society and mediated transactions not only between villages and towns, but those at the inter-village level as well. We do not know of any reliable statistical figure on the number of such markets in Mughal India or in precolonial India as a whole. A rough attempt, however, has been made by Stephen Blake to estimate the number of such markets in north India on the basis on the number of measured villages in the provinces of Agra, Delhi and Lahore in 1600. Blake's calculations show a total of 1502 'standard' and 834 'intermediate' marketing centres in the three provinces.[47] The former were preiodically held centres (*haats*) lying at the bottom of the marketing hierarchy and the latter were more regular markets (*bazaars*) serving a wider hinterland. If we take the estimate of the number of measured villages as made by Habib for 1700[48], the number of these centres would be 2862 and 854 (applying Blake's method of calculation, i.e. taking the number of standard centres ad 3% and that of intermediate centres as 1% of measured villages, and assuming that the percentage of such markets in Mughal India was constant over the 17th century). Such centres, needless to mention, were spread all over Mughal India.

In order to ascertain properly the role of these centres, alternatively called *haats* and *bazaars*, in the supply of goods in the empire and beyond, we have to ask the question: was the countryside the supplier of agricultural commodities only? We quote Tapan Raychaudhuri once again, "Manufacturing in Mughal India was predominantly a rural activity though most urban centres also had their artisan industries, especially production of certain luxury and semi-luxury goods. Only any exclusive concentration of secondary production in towns and cities with the countryside supplying the raw material—characteristic of mediaeval Europe—was not to be found."[49] A discerning reader cannot fail to notice the contradictory pull in this statment. Expressions such as 'predominantly a rural activity' and 'only an exclusive concentration of secondary production' cannot easily be reconciled and hence do not aid any conclusion.

We do not know of any flow of manufactured goods, manufactured in towns, from urban to rural areas—if there was any, it must have been insignificant—and therefore, the question of any exclusive concentration should not arise at all. To understand the matter somewhat clearly, we have to look at the degree and nature of urbanization and urban manufacturing in Mughal India. There can be no gainsaying that there was significant promotion of urbanization, and the growth of urbanization clearly indicates growing use of money, because the transfer of produce to urban areas definitely required the use of money and mediation by merchants. H.K. Naqvi, Gavin Hambly and Shireen Moosvi have studied the subject of urbanization in Mughal India. Hambly has identified four different types of urban centres. In the first category were those centres whose principal functions were administrative. To the second category belonged those centres that had a predominantly commercial and manufacturing character. The third category comprised the centres of pilgrimage. Finlly, there were those centres which developed and flourished because of some distinct manufacturing technique, craft skill or local commodity which ensured their ongoing prosperity.[50] From the studies of Naqvi and Moosvi, we are informed that there were quite a few manufacturing towns and cities such as Fatehpur Sikri, Gwalior, Lucknow, Alwar, Panipat, etc. and some other cities such as Lahore, Surat, Ahmadabad, Delhi and Agra, which had their own manufacturing establishments. Paper was exclusively an urban industry and various cotton goods and cotton fabrics were produced in urban areas. Urban production of textiles was most pronounced in the United Provinces.[51] Rauchaudhuri and Habib have provided excellent accounts of establishment of *karkhanas* and patronization of arts by noblemen living in cities. Habib has at the same time pointed out that the nobles did not always got their supplies from their *karkhanas*.[52] We may conclude that urban manufacturing developed in Mughal India very much unevenly, and that regional differences must not be lost sight of in evaluating the importance or urban manufacturing, or for that matter urban economic activity, in the empire as a whole. On the basis of the assumption that all manufactures consumed by the urban population were produced by urban labour, Shireen Moosvi has estimated the value of urban manufacturing of Mughal India to be 9.6% of its agricultural production.[53]

In order to examine the issue of urbanization in Mughal India somewhat more analytically, we believe that the two economic categories, commerce and manufacturing, should be distinguished. A centre of commerce may not necessarily be a centre of manufacturing. From Stewart Gordon's study of the town of Burhanpur, it seems that the city, besides being an administrative and militry centre, was a commercial centre as well, but it was by no means a manufacturing centre.[54] The city of Agra was more famous for its vast market than for its manufacturing. It should be recognized that urban manufacturing was not synonymous with urban marketing in manufactures in Mughal India. On the manufacture of cotton textiles in Bangal of the early 18th century, a distinguished student of the pre-colonial economy of Bengal has observed, "No doubt the European companies and to some extent, the Asian merchants, collected their cloth for export mainly at several marts and urban centrers but that too through a network of intermediaries whose agents procured the wares from the weavers or hats in the rural areas. Dacca, Kasimbazar, Malda, Hughli, Radhanagar, Santipur, Jugdea etc, were mainly the emporia rather than prominent weaving centers."[55] It can be easily surmised that before the start of the period of Company trading, the rural character of Bengal's textile manufacturing was no less pronounced, because Company trading should promote urbanization (and specialization), and that Bengal was arguably the premier manufacturing region of the Mughal empire. Sugar was also an important export commodity of Bengal and it was definitely a manufacturing item produced in the villages. Considered in view of the above, Shireen Moosvi's assumption that all manufactures for urban consumption were produced by urban labour seems to be a heroic one and hence her estimate highly exaggerated.

Our task, however, is not to criticize this or that assumption or estimate, but to ascertain the correct position of the countryside in the economy of Mughal India as a whole. Besides Bengal, there are other examples of rural areas supplying manufactures to towns. In the article of Grover we have referred to earlier, it is suggested that the countryside of Allahabad produced cotton cloth for Agra, Delhi and other places.[56] The weaving villages in the neighbourhood of Surat and Ahmadabad served as an important hinterland for Surat's export market.[57] Examples can be found from Bihar, where weavers from hinterland villages sold their raw cotton cloth in towns of lesser fame, while in big cities they sold it 'whited and cured'.[58] Such examples, which are at least as singnificant as to attract the attention of historians, must be excluded from the category of urban manufacturing. It follows that in Raychaudhuri's above-quoted comment on manufacturing in Mughal India, the first part, which suggests manufacturing to be a predominantly rural activity, is more apposite. It is true that there was a concentration of skilled craftsmen in urban areas, and hence the bulk of skill-intensive goods were produced in urban areas. But coarse goods, for example coarse cloth, were produced predominantly in rural areas, and they were exported in large quantities. If we take into account the entire productive spectrum of the rural areas, it may be concluded that the rural areas supplied not only food crops like cereals and pulses, or raw materials like cotton, but large quantities of manufactured items as well to urban areas. So it may be suggested that standard and intermediate marketing centres (rural *haats* and *bazaars*) of the countryside served as foundational markets in sustaining the flow of goods and money across the empire.

On the nature of currencies in circulation in these marketing centres, we can claim that non-imperial low-value currency media circulated predominantly in these centres. If it is a fact that the price of the copper *dam* rose and its minting declined substantially in the 17th century, then it can be concluded that in the miniscule transactions conducted at rural standard and intermediate marketing centres, where prices were generally lower than urban prices, a copper *dam* might have often proved too high for some transactions. Hence such transactions seemingly required a currency of still lower denomination.

Cowrie (small shell used as money), whose exchange value was many times lower than that of the *dam*, was well-suited to play this role. Tavernier, the French jeweller who toured the country extensively, saw the exchange of *cowries* with copper coins in Agra in 1665.[59] The destination of these *cowries* is, however, unreported. Given that the number of small-priced transactions in rural *haats* was far greater, it can be legitimately surmised that *cowries* penetrated these centres in a substantial measure. *Cowrie* use in Bengal merits a separate discussion because *cowrie* was considered synonymous with money in this province.

We have already argued that seeking a one-to-one correspondence between marketing of produce and revenue payment is not necessarily the best way of understanding rural monetization. That a process of increasing involvement of peasants and artisans in monetized exchanges was taking place in Mughal India is corroborated by historians' judgments. To quote Tapan Raychaudhuri once again, ".... very probably by the mid-eighteenth century the entire production for the long and medium-distance trade was dependent on artisans who were fully weaned from the *jajmani* system"[60] (the system of customary reciprocal exchange of goods and services among the inhabitants of a village or group of villages). This 'weaning' was definitely not a suddenly emerging phenomenon, but a process spanning many years and decades, and such a process clearly implied the growing involvement of artisans producing for medium and long-distance trade in monetized exchanges for procuring their necessities (raw materials and victuals). It can be inferred that with the gradual rise and growth of Company trading in Indian goods, this process gathered momentum. It also shows that there was growing monetization of the production economy. It is not, however, possible to quantify this growth. The role of rural marketing centres in the producers' involvement in monetized exchanges may be specifically underlined as follows: In some cases, the distinction between production for the local market and production for the distant market was blurred. In such cases, the producers used the local market both for the sale of their goods and for the purchase of their necessities. In others, where the transactions between the producer and the trader were conducted according to some pre-specified arrangements, the local rural market was used by the producer only for the purchase of necessities, i.e. victuals and raw materials, while the output was delivered to the contracting merchant.

The surplus taken out of the rural production economy travelled through inter-local, intra-regional and inter-regional networks of exchange owing to diversities in resource endownments and consumption needs. The concurrent exchange requirements generated a flow of money and merchandise throughout the empire and beyond. It is through this flow that the tie between revenue and trade was formed. An export sector resting on the ability of merchants to appropriate a part of the surplus out of the production economy and to sell this part to foreign customers nourished this flow and also expanded the scope of horizontal exchanges. This elaborate trading network set up a tie between various categories of merchants and producers.

In general, we can delineate three categories of market formations in Mughal India. The foundational markets were generally the rural market formations serving the needs of intra-local and inter-local exchanges as well as the flow of goods from rural to urban centres (it should be noted that often goods produced in one rural and urban centres, for example, the transportation of raw cotton from the Surat-Burhanpur axis to the cloth-producing countryside of Bengal). It should be noted that in Mughal India in general, there was no role of coastal trade in supplying the consumption needs of the population. So, *haats* and *bazaar* or *mandis* (standard and intermediate marketing centres) may legitimately be said to have played the foundational role in the supply of goods. The second type was the network of market formations located in urban centres serving the consumption needs of urban population. The third type was constituted by those markets that grew in India and abroad in response to external demand for Indian goods. Urban markets, however, were divided into various catagories, such as *mandis* (wholsale markets), *nakhsas* (daily markets), *katras* (enclosed markets).[61] There might have been some spatial overlapping between the markets of urban areas serving as administrative centres and the markets of port towns, but the functional distinction in their respective roles in the economy is clear enough.

This analytical division is somewhat at variance with K.N. Chaudhuri's threefold division of markets for Indian goods in the 17th and 18th centuries. To quote Chaudhuri, "If a functional hierarchy is constructed, at the apex would appear the great sea port markets, Surat, Masulipatnam and Hugli, along with Jedda, Mocha, Gomroon, Malacca, Achin and Canton, can be placed in such a hierarchy. In the second category were regional or provincial commercial towns, which served as entrepot for a smaller hinterland or area of influence. We have no difficulty in recognizing these places for India; they were Patna, Benares, Agra, Burhanpur, Lahore, Multan and many other towns of lesser frame. The third type of market was not located at a particular place or town but was rather a collection of small towns and villages forming a single unit and producing a single export commodity. By way of example, one can name Biana and Sarkhej for indigo, the Chapra district of Bihar for saltpeter, the raw silk-producing areas of Kasimbazar, the Dacca district for fine cotton textiles and so on."[62] It should be pointed out that the difference between Chaudhuri's and our categorization is one of emphasis, not of facts. The rationale of our categorization is twofold. First of all, if the connection between surplus appropriation and market formation is to be captured within a framework of functional hierarchy of markets, our generalized categories are seemingly more apposite. Second, it is well known that India's export and inland trade items consisted not only of specialized and finer items, but of non-specialized goods such as rice, coarse textiles, etc. as well. Our division takes into account this fact. Of course, K.N. Chaudhuri made this dividion in regard to the inter-regional and sea- borne trade. But it should be kept in mind that the so-called coarse goods, particlulary coarse cloth, also were in good demand in Asian markets. This is a well-attested historical fact.[63]

Merchants involved in the procurement of goods from the

foundational markets can be divided into two broad categories. One was the peddling traders who 'went from village to village with their pack bullocks, buying pieces of cloth from individual weavers and retailing their wares in the same fashion'.[64] The other were the more substantial merchants carrying their goods to distant markets and selling them either to urban or foreign customers or to more upper-level merchants. These merchants also were divided into various categories. Merchants selling their goods to foreign customers in overseas ports or overland trading places located abroad constituted one category and it is easily understandable that they procured their wares through their agents or lower-level merchants. Merchants dealing with foreign customers in Indian ports fell in another category. Merchants transacting with urban domestic customers constituted a third group. Of course, there were divisions within each category or group in terms of wealth and scale of operations. But it should be emphasized that all these mercantile practices were largely dependent on the countryside of Mughal India for the supply of goods.

The selling practices of peasants and artisans were related with the need to pay revenue and also to procure their necessities. The procuring merchant qua merchant was also under the compulsion to purchase from the producers and their representatives and so, there was an intertwining of interests. In an urban or overseas market, on the other hand, such an intertwining was absent. The growth of urbanization and urban commercial centres in consequence of the expansion of Mughal ruling establishments continuously enhanced the demand for goods and to that extent merchants stood to gain. It is through the vertical transfer of goods by way of intra-regional and inter-regional trade from merchandise-supplying hinterlands to urban centres of consumption and commerce as well as to port markets located in India and abroad that merchants could principally acquire their profits.

The members of the Mughal imperial bureaucracy, namely the imperial household and *mansabdars* and their dependents (troops, officials and other professionals) constituted mostly through imperial legal tender money. But we have to remember that merchants also had to procure humbler and coarser currency media in order to procure humbler and coarser currency media in order to procure merchandise from the rural marketing centres. *Cowrie* was only one of those media. A more thorough examination of the silver order can illuminate us more on the rold played by non-imperial exchange media in sustaining the flow of money and merchandise within the empire itself.

NON-IMPERIAL CURRENCIES IN THE EMPIRE

We have earlier argued that *cowrie* possibly played a role complementary to that of the silver rupee and its fractional piece *anna*, in the wake of the ascendancy of silver and decline in the pricer of copper. This view finds support in Fernand Braudel's observation that the *cowrie* came to replace copper, at least partly, as an item on the list of the imports of the Indian subcontinent in the early 17th century.[65] It should be noted that the closing decades of the 17th century witnessed a large-scale revival of copper imports, mainly from Japan.[66] From whatever empirical evidence we do have, there is no way of suggesting that with this revival, there was an increase in the production of Mughal copper coins. As the incidence of internal wars and rebellions in the empire grew, copper was increasingly used for the production of armaments. But the replacement of the copper *dam* by the silver *anna* and *cowrie* was only one aspect of the monetary situation of 17th century India. In order to have a fuller understanding, we have to look at the pattern of use of silver money more closely.

It is perhaps a mistake to equate the silver order with the domination of the imperial rupee (*rupayaa*). The most obvious illustration of it is the large-scale use of *mahmudi*, a coarser coin of Sultanic descent and with a value equivalent to about two-fifth of the rupee, in the inland and coastal trade of Gujarat.[67] According to Om Prakash, *mahmudi* was the only major non-Mughal coin that was allowed to circulate in Mughal India.[68] Here one should add some qualifications. Before the Mughal conquest of Gujarat and the setting up of an imperial mint in

Ahmadabad, *mahmudi* was the principal currency in settling Gujarat's trade balances with north India. The rupee began to replace *mahamudi* after the Mughal conquest of Gujarat and the establishment of an imperial mint in Ahmadabad.[69] But it is possible that the rupees minted in Ahmadabad were not sufficient to drive out *mahmudis* from local circulation. When the centre of coin production shifted to Surat, and Gujarat's foreign trade came to be centred round Surat instead of Cambay, there was a visible dearth of the supply of rupees for local circulation, although the Surat mint regularly turned out enormous quantities of Mughal rupees. The dearth of rupees is attributed to a flight of Surat rupees to upper India. It was not only by way of tribute. Much of Surat's goods came through upper India and Agra was a large market for them, as is corroborated by the finding of Shireen Moosvi that a bill drawn at Surat on Agra carried a high discount.[70] In the situation of the 17th century, it is conceivable that there was considerable physical movement of rupees from Surat to upper India. One need not try to estimate the representation of Surat rupees in imperial hoards in order to draw such a conclusion.

That is probably why the 'major exception' was allowed to circulate. It is interesting to note that here 'bad money' did not drive out 'good money' from circulation. In fact the distinction is irrelevant here because neither the state nor the merchants attached the same nominal value to the rupee and *mahamudi*.[71] On the fact of circulation of *mahmudi*, it should be added that in Gujarat, a non-minted humble currency medium, somewhat analogous to the *cowrie*, was in circulation. It was *badam*, bitter almond imported from Persia, having a market price somewhat higher than the *cowrie*.[72] It may be noted in passing that Gujarat was one of the highly commercialized regions of Mughal India. The gap between the demand for money and the supply of imperial legal tender, notwithstanding the imperial system of free minting, can be further illustrated with reference to the pattern of use of money in Mughal Bengal.

It should be noted that although the formal conquest of Bengal took place in 1576, 'no Mughal coinage of Bengal provenance is known prior to A.H. 1002 (A.D. 1593-4)'[73] But gradually, imperial mints were set up at Rajmahal, Dacca and Karimabad (Murshidabad), and the imperial monetary system was sought to be imposed. But here too various other rupee coins, namely the Madras rupee and different kinds of *Arcot* rupees flowed in via the channels of Company trading since the mid-17th century and ultimately came to be accepted in the local internal trade of the districts of eastern Bengal, thereby lending a pluralistic character to the monetary order, which became a problem to the English East India Company's government when they took over the administration of Bengal.[74] We may also refer to the use of the *Narainy* rupee, accepted by the Mughals at the time of the Mughal conquest of Coochbihar in 1661. The conquest of Coochbihar was, however, largely formal and there is no evidence that it was even more than a tributary state in relation to the Mughals.[75] The *Narainy* rupee, minted by the Raja of Coochbihar, was current throughout north Bengal. And finally, we can refer to the vigorous Bengal-Maldives trade in which the *cowrie* shell was the overwhelming import item.[76] In the case of Bengal too, it was the dearth of supply of good money that allowed the so-called 'bad money' to circulate, but none drove out the other.

This brief discussion highlights a point : within two commercially most significant regions of the Mughal empire, namely Bengal and Gujarat, the pattern of money use had a significant measure of difference from the imperial trimetallic system. This roughly corresponds to Pierre Vilar's profound obsrvation on the monetary system in the Deccan and South, "Everywhere there was a dual system with a current coin which was more or less fiduciary (i.e., with no guaranteed intrinsic value and taking many forms), and a strong currency accepted in large-scale trading."[77] The correspondence of the pattern of use of money in Bengal and Gujarat with that in the South is rough in the sense that the *cowrie* currency that was used in low-value exchanges throughout Bengal had a uniform character; it did not assume 'many forms'.

But how can the departure from the usual system of trimetallism be explained? One explanation might be that these two regions lay somewhat in the frontier area of the empire, and that is why the Mughal imperial system was difficult to enforce. But a geographical explanation is not always a very happy one. Another and more plausible explanation might be in terms of the degree of commercialization. Bengal and Gujarat were the two premier commercialized regions of the empire and the imperial mints could not satisfy the demand for money, hence the pattern and scale of use of money transcended the imperial monetary order.

We should be careful to note that this dualistic monetary system functioned within the context of a growing exchange between the hinterlands and urban centres of commerce. In this broad exchange process, the humble and crude currency media entered into exchanges with the 'strong'currencies with guaranteed intrinsic worth.

FOREIGN TRADE AND MONEY SUPPLY

It is now common knowledge that from view point of supply of monetary substance, the monetary system of pre-colonial India (including Mughal India) was very much dependent on import. Gold, silver, copper, the *cowrie, badam*—all of were, in general, products of India's external trade. Here again it should be emphasized that this dependence on imports implied a demand for these metallic and non-metallic substances in India. On the other hand, India was the exporter of a wide variety of goods such as cotton and silk goods, rice, opium, saltpeter, indigo, etc. In the light of this fact we may try to locate India' position in the international economy and to explain her position in relation to her trading partners. Here we should again emphasize that since those substances were commodities, their import into India should not be treated as meeting deficits in balance of payments on the part of India's trading partners.

It should be made clear at the outset that the chief source of the acoumulation of mercantile wealth in Mughal India was not her foreign trade. It may be argued, on the other hand, that through the process of transfer of real surplus to the non-producing classes and throgh the horizontal transfer of goods from one set of producers to another, a part of the physical surplus remained in the hands of merchants, which they disposed of in foreign markets in response to the demand for Indian goods abroad. This is not to suggest that those goods that could not be sold domestically were marketed through the channel of foreign trade. What is emphasized instead is that a part of the national product accrued to the mercantile classes by way of internal trade, and this part was sold to foreign customers in exchange of precious metals, other metallic and non-metallic substances. But this acquistion of surplus took place through the channels of internal trade. Foreign trade served to convert this surplus into money wealth. What however needs to be considered is how the gains from Indian merchants' participation in international trade were distributed.

The trading network involving Indian goods and merchangs had, however, a number of specificities, which should be properly noted. About the relatively less prominant *cowrie* trade, it should be pointed out that Indian as well as European merchants and companies brought these shells directly from the Maldives. The Indian merchants' *cowrie* trade was bilateral, while that of the Europeans was multilateral. The Maldives *cowries* bought by Europeans were also shipped to Europe, to find their way to West Africa. Second, the silver and gold of the New World that found their way to India reached Europe first and was then employed in India trade. We do not know of anything that suggests and direct imports of the New World silver and gold to India. Again, the English East India Company's imports from India were much more Europe-bound than those of the Dutch who traded in Indian goods with Ceylon, Japan and the East Indies.[78] The Dutch East India Company directly brought not only siver, but huge quantities of copper as well into India as part of its multilateral trading plan. Again, we do not know of any Indian ship sailing to Japan, Europe, Mexico or Brazil. The Dutch East India Company used to directly bring Japanese silver and copper into India as part of its multilateral trading plan. Out of all these specificities, however, emerges one generality. India was principally an exporter of manufactured and agricultural products, and an importer of precious metals and other monetary substances.

At least one authority has argued that the pattern of Indo-European trade can be explained by the theory of comparative advantage.[79] It is difficult to accept this proposition for two reasons. First of all, the Indo-European trade was by no means bilateral, as we have explained above. Second, there is no evidence to suggest that India was a producer of silver, albeit at a higher cost. So, this theory is not empirically terstable at all. Besides, the Ricardian theory does not consider the question of demand (it may be noted that in classical political economy in general, demand played a passive role).[80] Europe might find it convenient to send precious metals to Asia to pay for her imports, but one has to understand why India should purchase them. So, there remains the need for an alternative framework with a better explanatory value, a framework that takes into consideration the demand factor as well. The theory of 'vent for surplus' might be invoked, but it has its own problems, because it is also a supply-centred theory. The outflow of silver and gold from Europe into Asia, including India, is patently inexplicable in terms of it because in Europe, such outflows created considerable monetary instability, and Europe had to seek a solution in the circulation of 'bad money', credit money and paper currencies. Europe did not have, in this sense, a surplus of precious metals. Besides, there was widerspread production and of counterfeit coins.[81] So the need remains for investigating the areas of demand within a broader framework of multilateral trade. Here one caveat should be introduced. Indo-European trade was only one part of Mughal India's or, for that matter, pre-colonial India's foreign trade. The trade with central Asia and the Middle East at the initiative of Indian and other Asian merchants was equally prominent. The import of horses, precious metals and *badam* from Persia should be noted in this connection. When Indian maritime merchants could sell their goods directly at Asia's trading ports and to local merchants, this gain was conceivably favourable to them. But European companies controlled the sea-lanes to Europe. Besides, there was growing European domination over Asian waters. To the extent that this happened, the gains were unequally distributed, with the Indian merchants being at the receiving end. Indian merchants' maritime trade in the 17th century came to be concentrated in the Red Sea and Persian Gulf,[82] except, however, for the trade with the Maldives.

In short, it would not be too heroic to assume that the gradual rise and growth of Europeans in Asians waters severely constrained the operations of Indian overseas merchants. On the other hand, the operation of the European companies in Indian ports and their consequent needs of short-term finance facilitated the activities of another kind of merchants, i.e. those specializing in financial dealings. As we shall see later, the high demand for credit in relation to supply served to maintain a high rate of interest in at least on major commercial region, i.e. Bengal, and this high demand was significantly fuelled by the trading activities of the European Companies.

POLITY, ECONOMY AND MERCHANTS

We may now turn to another aspect of the Mughal economy, namely the relation between the state and merchants. This relation, it is needless to mention, could not remain static over time, and so, we have to consider whether there was any noteworthy change in it. It may be noted at the outset that with growth of trade, the role of merchants too grows and develops. At the outset, we should disabuse ourselves of the notion that the Mughals were in the habit of fleecing merchants indiscriminately. Mughal rulers were able to understand that the maintenance of their rule over such a vast areas required transfer of goods and money over ling distances, and this was simply not possible without the intermediacy of merchants, particularly more substantial merchants. Moreover, the Mughal emperors and prices, *subadars* and *mansabdars* often showed deep interest in water-borne trade.[83] It should be realized that the former was far more important. The prosperity of the Mughal establishment depended primarily, however, on agricultural surplus, not on commerce. Since the Mughal nobility did not depend in any significant way on the revenue to the acquired from trade, they did not have to tax merchants, highly, let alone fleece them.[84] As one authority pointed out succinetly, the oriental despot could be despotic if he chose, but he could not then be a very effective rulers.[85] But they could not dispense with the services of merchants, not as revenue payers, but as the suppliers of goods. It might be that there were cases of fleecing, but that was not a ubiquitous affair and did not hamper commercial activities in general. The point of debate is whether merchants were crucial in deciding the solution of political equations.

Here we can in all fairness refer to a debate between Karen Leonard and John F. Richards. Leonard suggested that the shift in loyalty on the part of large merchants and bankers ('great firms') was crucial in explaining the decline of the empire. John F. Richards took exception to this and argued that the economic merchanism devised by the Mughals was basically one of a huge state machinery in control of the resources and although the Mughals used the services of bankers for dispersal of resources, the stability of empire was not crucially dependent on the services of these great firms.[86] The debate contains much valuable information and gives rise to important questions.

First of all, it is apparent that merchants' and bankers' importance to the rulers as sources of credit and mangers of monetary transfers grew over time. As the extent of monetization grew and as the Mughal ruling classes became increasingly dependent on cash, merchants' services became more and more essential for the transfer of goods and money. Merchants were not certainly as important in 1600 as they were one century later. The second point is why merchants shifted their loyalty to regional powers and European Companies and moved away from the Mughal nobility. Was it because merchants and bankers began to lose faith in the Mughal ruling establishment that regional powers grew? Is it not more correct to say that the merchants and bankers shifted their alignment to regional powers when they found the empire in decline? When the spectre of a declining empire and consequently a decaying nobility looms large, it is quite natural that seeking fresh pastures for market is more profitable. It is not only possible but also probable that this shift hastened the decline of the empire, but to raise one contributory factor to the status of the principal explanatory variable, to the focal point of a theory is seemingly to mistake the symptom for the reason. After all, we should remember that the prosperity of the empire was due mainly to its agricultural wealth, not to trade, and that the internecine quarrel for appropriation of this wealth, and the over exploitation of the peasantry and consequent peasant revolts were a stark reality in the late 17th and early 18th centuries.[87]

If the merchants' importance had grown over time, it must have been by exploiting the vast inland and external markets that were undoubtedly fostered by Mughal stability. It is also reasonable to suppose that the vast Mughal establishment, i.e. the *mansabdars,* their troops and officials, the imperial household, their troops, dependents and other professional men formed the demand side of quite substantial urban markets (whether Indian merchants' capital, robbed of this market, had to atrophy in the wake of the decline of the empire is a different question). The external demand for Indian goods was also another source of mercantile profits. What needs to be understood is that merchants came to emerge as a conspicuous class of surplus appropriators in the course of time and gained a measure of autonomy that enabled them to survive in the aftermath of the imperial decline. The usual models of the pre-colonial economy of India, where the impact of foreign trade on the economy has been discussed, have in general underplayed this phenomenon. If merchants had remained in a static position, having only a servitor role acting as appendages to a surplus acquisition mechanism based on reciprocity—one might be tempted to call it market-less trade[88]—such underplaying would be justified. But the rise of prominent banking firms and the emergence of bankers as creditors to the nobility highlights the importance of studying mercantile operations with at least some degree of emphasis. This is not to attribute to the merchants and mercantile wealth the crucial causal significance in the decline of the Mughal empire; this is only to argue that the role of the merchants, goods as well as money merchants, in the economy grew in the changing landscape of the Indian subcontinent. This increased role was one factor in the loss of independence of the successor regimes and the arrival of the East India Company as the ruler, in consequence of which the merchants also lost their autonomy and became subordinates to the new rulers.

In his remarkably insightful work, *Theory of Economic History*, Prof. J.R. Hicks remarked that the Mughal empire was an example of classical bureaucracy. He defined classical bureaucracy as a system in which command elements predominated. In this system the process of transfer of surplus was logically independent of trade. Merchants here have a dependent status in the sense that they have no autonomous economic role to play and have just to reproduce themselves unchangeably.[89] The same position, without the very mention of merchants, was taken somewhat earlier by an eminent social-anthropologist in the following language:

"In a large kindom with a moderately powerful center, such as the Mughal Empire was at times, there was a hierarchy of redistrbutive centers with the village grain heap at the botton and the provincial governors maintained their own storchouses, retaining a share and passing on the remainder of the level above. In regard to grain, the whole political and social structure was founded on redistribution."[90]

This view apparently contains some truth because the huge Mughal establishment spread over a vast territory acted as a large customer of goods and services produced by peasants and artisans and procured by merchants. But the question is whether merchants came to gain some autonomous position, although they did not have the state power in their hands. Certainly merchants' independence and initiative did not proceed so far as to allow them to conceive of something like a mercantile city-state, which Hicks considered as the natural upshot of the growth of independent mercantile activities.

It may be considered worthwhile to consider the applicability of Karl Polanyi's theory of market-less trade in this context. Karl Polanyi's writings have exercised much influence on the theories of the market because he had explicitly examined the possible interdependence among money, power and social stratification. In market-less trade, trade is not dictated by prices. The prices are not set by bargaining (in the Smithian sense), and exchange takes place at set rates. In Europe, the market was promoted by the state. Deliberate state action cleared the way for a national market. Then the state stepped aside and at the next stage, the market became self-regulating. A self-regulating, or price-regulated merket, which represents a basic separation between the economic and the political sphere, is thus seen not as a natural but a historical category. The emergence of the price-making market is thus seen as a historical departure, the outcome of a 'Great Transformation'. Market-less trade, according to Polanyi, is broadly of two types, gift trade and administered trade. Gift trade contains considerable ceremonial and ritualistic elements, while in administered trade, exchange is geared to the needs of the state and is negotiated through government-controlled channels.[91]

Of course, Polanyi's notion of a separation between the economic and political sphere can be subjected to a good deal of criticism, considering the break brought about by Karl Marx in conceptualizing the social relations in an economy of generalized commodity production. But possibly, Polany's examination of the socio-historical movement that brought the phenomenon of market into being has some merits, at least in the sense that it has established that, like all other economic categories, the market is also a historical category, subject to a process of historical evolution, and that the market has its own social dimensions that need to be studied separately, not just as a site of exchange.

A scrutiny of the applicability of Polanyi's thesis in the context of Mughal India, or pre-colonial India in general must proceed with some degree of care. First of all, there was the influence of custom, tradition religion and motivations for tolls and taxes in the formation of marketplaces.[92] This denotes something different from price-making markets in the economic sense. Second, there was at least a partial correlation between surplus extraction and marketing of goods. When peasants sell their produce after harvest in order to meed the compulsion of tax-payment, the scope of bargaining is limited, and in this sense, *haats* and local *bazaars* do not conform to the type of self-regulating markets.

On the other hand, there are distinct indications of growth in the production of cash crops, which imply a growing motive for gain on the part of direct producers. More important, there was considerable speculation in urban and export markets and adjustment of supply and demand on the basis of experience.[93] Third, as we have argued earlier, there was the rise of big private urban-based goods and money merchaants. All these show that commerce in Mughal India went somewhat beyond the limits of market-less trade, at least in the big urban markets. We cannot however, equate them with modern competitive markets and have to make allowance for imperfections characteristic of pre-modern markets.

DECLINE OF THE EMPIRE AND COMMERCE

The reasons for the decline of the Mughal empire have been discussed by historians like Irfan Habib, Satish Chandra and Athar Ali, Gautam Bhadra and the like, and from a different viewpoint by Muzaffar Alam and C.A. Bayly.[94] Habib, Chandra and Ali have pointed out the crisis of the *jagirdari* system, manifested in the increasing gap between assessment (*jama*) and collection (*hasil*) as one principal reason. Ali has drawn attention to the internecine quarrel among the *mansabdars* for *jagirs* (revenue assignments) and the scarcity of them.[95] Habib referred also to the crisis of over exploitation and peasant revolts. Alam and Bayly, on the other hand, tried to understand the crisis in terms of the relation between the centre, and the regional power groups. It is probable that both these versions had elements of truth, as there is some evidence in favour of each. The point is whether and how much Indian merchant capital had to suffer owing to the loss of market consequent upon the decline of the Mughal bureaucracy. In the sphere of coin production, the impact of this decline was retrogressive, at least in upper India. The Mughal mints were farmed out and the supervision was lax. The Mughal *rupayaa* was in circulation, but it was subjected to continuous debasement.[96] More important is the question whether commerce and money use itself went into a decline following the collapse of the empire. The proposition of atrophy was put forward by Habib as far back as 1969 in the following words, "....denied, during the eighteenth century, the large market that it had been provided with by the Mughal Empire, merchant capital had no choice but to atrophy".[97] The stability brought about by Mughal rule was certainly conducive to trade and the huge Mughal establishments at the supra-village level provided a large market for agricultural goods as well as manufacture. The Mughal emphasis on uniformity of coins was also favourable to merchants engaged in the transfer of goods over long distances within the empire.

So, it is tempting to accept the suggestion that merchants' operations suffered a severe setback in consequence of the decline. Some accounts, for example, those given by Ashin Dasgupta regarding Surat, seem to lend credibility to this notion.[98] However, there remains the important question as to whether the regional kingdoms that developed in the wake of the Mughal decline needed the services of merchants or not . Another important question is whether the Mughal decay had a proportionately adverse effect on all types of commerce and crafts. The research done by C.A. Bayly has shown that with the rise of regional centres of power, along with the re-establishment of some sort of stability, there was substantial reorientation of trade routes and there might not have been a decline of trade.[99] The Maratha conquest of Malwa also suggests something like this.[100] Much earlier, B.R. Grover also opined, "During the eighteenth century, the ruination of the Mughal nobility and the aristocracy resulted in lack of partonage for industrial goods. But this affected the state owned *karkhanas* located in the cities rather than rural commercial production. Owing to political upheavals and chaotic intermissions, there was considerable reshuffling in the territorial jurisdictions of local chief and *zamindar* families. But this did not affect the consumption or patronage of the indigenous rural production since the newly established *zamindar* families patronized the local craftsmanship as the old families had done."[101] Grover did not discuss the rise of new centres of power and their resurrecting impact on commerce, but from his observation, one can have the impression that the role of rural commercial production in the economy of the empire has to be considered and the notion of 'atrophy' to be re-examined.

The debate is continuting, and it is difficult for non-historians to take sides. But there are some too obvious examples that can be brought in for examination. Bayly's study is concerned exaclusively with north India. For Bengal, there are examples that are more glaring. Some money merchants, such as the legendary banking house of Jagat Seths, rose to a position of maximum prosperity in a period when the last powerful Mughal emperor, Aurangzeb, had already died and new, independent regional kingdoms were emerging.[102] There arose large goods merchants like Khwaia Wajid and Omichand. Murshidabad, the capital of the nawabs of Bengal, was a rich and prosperous city, as well as a large centre of commerce till the early period of the Company's *diwani* (1765). Some individual merchants, such as Surat's Abdul Gafur, might have gone into oblivion, but is is difficult to accept that the merchant community as a whole lost largely in terms of wealth. Marchants like Khwaja Wajid and Omichand of Bengal attained their prosperity when the Mughal empire was very much in the process of disintegration and decline.[103] In fact, there are reasons to believe that Surat's decline partly helped Bengal in retaining her commercial eminence. Hence one cannot accept the atrophy thesis so easily; it is definite that it should be seriously qualified.

It is interesting that some noted historians, who have disputed the atrophy thesis with much force, have advocated the notion of a general continuity till the early 19th century. It is also problematic to subscribe to this notion without reservation. Similarity in methods of business operation does not suggest an essential continuity. What needs to be examined is whether the character of indigenous merchants and bankers in relation to the state remained essentially the same under the new dispensation, which emerged in the wake of the giant strides of the English Company in India's political scene. Put alternatively, the political economy of commerce in the two periods has to be carefully studied and the differences as well similarities, apparent and real, seriously examined. The same examination is necessary in the case of rural potentates like *zamindars.* We have to study if the position of these potentates underwent any significant change under the rule of the English East India Company. If such a change is dicerned, it becomes problematic to accept the thesis of so-called continuity.

To revert to the nature of monetary media in circulation, we may recapitulate our earlier observation—that the need of money use and growth of commerce allowed many non-imperial and non-minted media to circulate. It is futile to state that the demand was matched by supply. The supply of currency turned out by imperial mints was hopelessly short of demand, particularly in more commercialized regions and this shortage was overcome by allowing non-imperial currency media to curculate. Here we must remember that notwithstanding the system of free minting, the supply of money was demand-determined, subject only to the number and capacity of imperial mints. The silver *larins* and *reals* had to be converted into Mughal coins, but currencies that were in used traditionally since the pre-Mughal days had to be accommodated. So, statements like 'Mughal currency had currency'[104] can be accepted only after some qualifications.

How does we interpred this symbiosis? Should we portray it as some kind of dualism? Frank Perlin has argued against this notion, pointing out that imports of silver and cowries represented two sides of the same market economy and that they did not represent two different sectors.[105] His argument has good ground. But if we consider the fact that the monetary media in circulation in Mughal India can be divided into two categories, imperial and non-imperial, we can conceive of a dualistic framework. These non-imperial media like *cowrie, mahmudi* or *Narainy* were traditionally used currencies, interacting with state-sponsored ones and facilitating the transfer of goods from the countryside to large urban markets. One can find an analogy with the Lewis type model of a dual economy. In such models the traditional sector evaporates with a fast rate of capital accumulation.[106] In our conception of monetary dualism, the humble, non-state currency media went into insignificance when the state assumed some sort of hegemony in the monetary sphere. This hegemony was achieved by the colonizing state of the British after a long process of struggle and coercion. Alternatively, we may call the pre-colonial monetary order a pluralistic monetary order. This pluralism in the pattern of money use becomes more apparent as we move on to study south India, where gold and not silver was the dominant currency metal through centuries, and where the polity was much more decentralized.

NOTES AND REFERENCES

1. Raychaudhuri, Tapan. "Agrarian System of Mughal India." A Review Essay, Enquiry, 1965. Reprinted in *The Mughal State.* Eds. Muzaffar Alam and Sanjay Subrahamanyam. India: OUP, 1997 : 282.
2. Habib, Irfan. "Agrarian Relations and Land Revenue." In *Cambridge Economic History of India.* Vol. 1. Eds. Irfan Habib and Tapan Raychaudhuri. Orient Longman, 1982 : 236–38.
3. Subrahmanyam, Sanjay. "Introduction" to Idem. Ed. *Money and Market in India* 1100–1700. O.U.P., 1994 : 19–20. Om Prakash: Foreign Merchants and Indian Mints in the Seventeenth and the early Eighteenth Century in *The Imperial Monetary System in Mughal India.* Ed. J.F. Richards, O.U.P., 1987: 172.
4. Haider, Najaf. "Precious Metal Flows and Currency Circulation in the Mughal Empire." *J.E.S.H.O.* 39, no. 3 (1996) : 304–05.
5. For a reasonably good account, vide John S. Deyell. "The Development of Akbar's Currency System and Monetary Integration of the Conquered Kingdoms" Ed. J.F. Richards : Op.cit., 13–67.
6. Habib, Irfan. "Monetary System and Prices". *C.E.H.I.* 1, Ch. XII (1) : 360–62.
7. Pradash, Om. "On Coinage in Mughal India". *I.E.S.H.R.* 25, no. 3, Om Prakash, after examining the available information, has suggested, "All these details establish beyond doubt that there is a sharp reduction in the rate of seigniorage from 5 per cent at the end of the sixteenth century to 3.37 per cent by the end of the seventeenth and to a further 2.5 per cent in the eighteenth century". Ibid, 481.
   Najaf Haider also expresses the same opinion. Vide Haider *Precious Metal Flows* .... 335.
8. Sher Shah ruled during 1540–45. The spurt in the inflow of American silver began later.

9. Habib, Irfan. A System of Trimetallism..... 147–156.
10. For a modern study, vide Pierre Vilar. *A History of Gold and Money*, N.L.B., 1976, Ch. 12, 103–114.
11. A summary of this view is to be found in Habib's *A System of Trimetallism....* 137–170.
12. Atwell, William S. "International Bullion Flows and the Chinese Economy, Circa 1530–1650". *Past and Present*, ..., no. 95 (1982): 120–127.
13. Habib, Irfan. ....A System of Trimetallism...., Table 3.
14. Richards, J.F. "The Mughal State Finance and the Pre-modern World Economy". *C.S.S.H.* 23, no. 3 (1981) : 297.
15. For a summary of these findings, Fischer, David Hackett. *The Great Wave; Price Revolutions and the Rhythm of History.* New York : O.U.P., 2004. In the Spanish case, Fischer has observed, "In Spain, where the impact of American treasure was comparatively large, the pace of inflation actually lagged behind other parts of Europe. Moreover, the largest proportionate increases in Spanish prices occurred during the first half of the sixteenth century—not the second half, when American treasure had its greatest impact." Ibid, 82.
16. Hasan, Aziza. "The Silver Currency Output of the Mughal Empire and Prices in India during the 16th and 17th centuries". *I.E.S.H.R.* 6, no. 1 (1969) : 85–116.
    Moosvi, Shireen : *The Economy of the Mughal Empire c 1595, A Statistical Study.* O.U.P., ...: 351–74.
17. Habib, Irfan. *A System of Trimetallism.....*, Table 2.
18. Moosvi, Shireen. "The Silver Influx, Money Supply, Prices and Revenue Extraction in Mughal India". *J.E.S.H.O.* 31, no. 1 (1987): 47–94.
19. Moosvi, Shireen. Ibid, 87–88.
20. Idem : The Indian Economic experience 1600–1900 : A Quantitative Study in *The Making of History—Essays Presented to Irfan Habib.* Delhi: Tulika, 2000 : 336–339.
21. Glamann, Kristoff. "European Trade 1500–1700" in *The Fontana Economic History of Europe—The Sixteenth and Seventeenth Centuries.* Ed. C.M. Cipolla. Glasgow: Collins/Fontana, 1974 : 490–91.
22. Moosvi, Shireen. *Silver Influx, Money Supply ....* 86– 87.
    Habib, Irfan. *A System of Trimetallism....* 150.
23. Deyell, John S. "Long Term Trends in the Production of Copper Coins in the Mughal Empire, Table III, in *The Imperial Monetary System of Mughal India.* Ed. J.F. Richards.

24. Perlin, Frank. Money use in Late Precolonial India and International Trade in Currency Media, Ibid, 253.
25. Atwell, William S. International Bullion Flows and the Chinese Economy...., Table 1. Atwell's calculations suggest that the relative price of gold in relation to silver in China was lower than in the Spanish empire during 1566–1643, and yet he observes that a small quantity of gold went into circulation. Irfan Habib's findings suggest that silver price of gold was higher in India than in China during the same period. Vide Habib : Monetary System and Prices, Table 9.
26. Haider, Najaf. Precious Metal flows and Currency Circulation... pp. 353–55.
27. Moosvi, Shireen. Silver Influx, Money Supply... p. 88.
28. Prakash, Om. *The Dutch East India Company and the Economy of Bengal*, 1630–1720. O.U.P., 1988 : 127–130.
29. Prakash, Om. Ibid, pp. 248–53. Sushil Chaudhuri. *Trade and Commercial Organization in Bengal*, 1640–1720. Firma K.L. Mukhopadhyay, Kolkata, 1976 : 241–48.
For a detailed scrutiny of the 18th century price data, vide Chaudhuri, Sushil. *From Prosperity to Decline—Bengal in the Eighteenth Century*. Delhi : Manohar, 1995 : 278–305.
30. Habib, Irfan. Monetary System and Prices, 376–77.
Moosvi, Shireen. *The Economy of the Mughal Empire* ...., p. 373.
Idem : A Note on the Interest Rates in the Seventeenth-Eighteenth Centuries, in *Mondy and Credit in Indian History*. Ed. Amiya Kumar Bagchi. Delhi: Tulika, 2002 : 84–92.
31. Habib, Irfan. Monetary System and Prices... 366–77.
32. For an excellent exposition of this argument, vide Bhaduri, Amit. *Macroeconomics: The Dynamics of Commodity Production*. Macmillan, 1986: 90–96.
33. Braudel, F. and F.C. Spooner. Prices in Europe from 1450 to 1750 in *Cambridge Economic History of Europe*. Vol. IV. Eds. E.E. Rich and C.H. Wilson. 378–486.
34. Habib, Irfan. "Population". *C.E.H.I.* 1, Ch. VI : 167–171.
35. Moosvi, Shireen. *The Economy of the Mughal Empire* .... 375–380.
36. Habib, Irfan. Potentialities of Capitalist Development in Mughal India repriented in Idem : *Essays in Indian History*. Delhi : Tulika, 1995 : 231–32.
37. Blake, Stephen. "The Structure of Monetary Exchange in North India". The Provinces of Agra, Delhi and Lahore in 1600 in *The Imperial Monetary System of Mughal*. Ed. J.F. Richards. Blake has tried to estimate the sums of money in circulation only from the

tax collection figures of the *Ain* and then has suggested in a rather peculiar fashion, "it would only have been in the circles headed by the larger cities, where commercial activity was highly developed, that the volume of money in circulation would have greatly exceeded the estimates derived from the *Ain*". Ibid, 134.

J.F. Richards : Official Revenues and Money Flows in a Mughal Province, in the same volume.

38. Raychaudhuri, Tapan. The Agrarian System ....., 280–82.
39. Idem : Inland Trade, *C.E.H.I.* I, Ch. XI : 327.
40. Grover, B.R. "An Integrated Pattern of Commercial Life in the Rural Society of North India during the Seventeenth and Eighteenth Centuries". Reprinted in *Money and Market in India* 1100–1700. Ed. Sanjay Subrahmanyam. ..... : ...., 222–24.
41. Sen, Sudipta. *The Empire of Free Trade.* Philadelphia: Pensylvania University Press, 1998, Chapter 1, passim.
42. Raychaudhuri, Tapan. Inland Trade, p. 325. It should be remembered that zamindars in Bengal had a fair measure of autonomy, and not always collected revenue according to Mughal norms.
43. Ibid, 358.
44. Idem : "The State and the Economy". *C.E.H.I.* I, Ch. VII (1) : 174.
45. Idem : "The Eighteenth Century Background". *C.E.H.I.* 2, Ch. I, Orient Longman, 1984 : 15–16.
46. Haider, Najaf. The Monetary Basis of Credit and Banking Instruments of the Mughal Empire. *Money and Credit...* Ed. Amiya Bagchi. 60.
47. Blake, Stephen. The Structure of Monetary Exchange in North India.... 119–21. Blake's estimate is crude in the sense that the applies the ratio between the number of marketing centres and measured villages obtained in China in 1800 to Mughal India in 1600. He admits that China in 1800 was more urbanized than India in 1600, but argues that 'using these percentages seems the best way of obtaining a rough approximation' of the number of marketing centres at the lowest and intermediate levels. Vide Ibid, 120.
48. Habib, Irfan. *The Agrarian System of Mughal India.* Bombay : Asia Publishing House, 1963 : 4.
49. Raychaudhuri, Tapan. "Non-agricultural Production". *C.E.H.I.* 1, CH. X(1) : 278.
50. Hambly, Gavin. "Towns and Cities." *C.E.H.I.* 1, Ch. XIV(1) : 434–35.

51. Naqvi, H.K. *Urbanization and Urban Centres under the Great Mughals, Institute for Advanced Studies.* Simla: 1971 : 140–41. Idem : *Urban Centres and Industries in Upper India,* 1556–1603. Bombay: Asia Publishing House, 1982 : 137–50. Moosvi, Shireen. *The Economy of the Mughal Empire* .... 299–321.
52. Habib, Irfan. Potentialities.... 240–248. Raychaudhuri, Tapan. The State and the Economy .... 180–81.
53. Moosvi, Shireen. Ibid, 306–07.
54. Gordon, Stewart. "Burhanpur; Entrepot and Hinterland, 1650–1720". *I.E.S.H.R.* 25, no. 3, 425–42.
55. Chaudhuri, Sushil. *From Prosperity to Decline....,* 135–36.
56. Grover, B.R. An Integrated Pattern of Commercial Life in the Rural Society ..... 234–35.
57. Arasaratnam, Sinnappa. *Maritime Trade in India in the Seventeenth Century.* O.U.P., 1997 : 83–84. Dasgupta, Ashin. "Trade and Politics in Eighteenth Century India". Reprinted in *The Mughal State.* Ed. Alam and Subrahmanyam. 370.
58. Sarkar, Smritikumar. "Social Organization of Artisan Production; Changing Role of the Market, Technology and Merchant Creditor—Eighteenth to Twentieth Centuries" in *Economic History of India From the Seventeenth to the Nineteenth Centuries.* Ed. Binay Chaudhuri. Delhi : Centre for Studies in Civiliations, 2005 : 141. This example is of the year 1620.
59. Tavernier, Jean Baptiste. *Travels in India,* Book 1. Trl. V., Ball, Delhi : Munshiram Manoharlal, 1995 : 22.
60. Raychaudhuri, Tapan. "Non-agricultural Production". *C.E.H.I.* 1, Ch. X(1) : 281.
61. For a brief, but good study of north Indian markets, Vide Ramesh Chandra Sharma. "Aspects of Business in Northern Indian in the Seventeenth Century" in *Essays in Medieval Indian Economic History.* Ed. Satish Chandra. Delhi : Munshiram Manoharlal, 1987.
62. Chaudhuri, K.N. "Markets and Traders in India during the Seventeenth and Eighteenth Centuries". Reprinted in *Money and Market in India.* Ed. Sanjay Subrahmanyam, 271.
63. Bhadra, Gautam. *Mughal Juge Krishi Arthaniti O Krishak Bidroha* (The Agrarian Economy and Peasant Revolts in the Muthal Era). Kokata : Subarnarekha, 1991 : 87–88 and 102–103.
64. Chaudhuri, K.N. Markets and Traders... 263.
65. Braudel, Fernand. *Capitalism and Material Life.* Glasgow: Collins/ Fontana, 1974 : 337.

66. Habib, Irfan. A System of Trimetallism... 150.
    Prakash, Om. *The Dutch East India Company and the Economy of Bengal* .... Table 5.2.
67. Tavernier, Jean Baptiste. *Travels in India,* Book 1. 21–22.
    Richards, J.F. Official Revenue and Money Flows in a Mughal Province ...., 194.
68. Prakash, Om. "On Coinage in Mughal India". *I.E.S.H.R.* 25, no. 4 (1988) : 477.
69. Deyell, John S. "The Development of Akbar's Currency System and Monetary Integration of the Conquered Kingdoms" in *The Imperial Monetary System in Mughal India.* Ed. Richards. 27–28.
70. Moosvi, Shireen. "Gujarati Ports and their Hinterlands". In *Ports and their Hinterlands in India.* Ed. Indu Banga. Delhi : Manohar, 1992 : 129.
71. Frank Perlin has attempted such an analysis in his "Monetary Revolution and Societal Change", in Perlin, *The Invisible City,* Ashgate and Hampshire, 1992, 345–348. Perlin seemingly considers the circulation of *mahmudi* instead of rupee as an example of 'Gresham on his head'. We consider the question irrelevant because the nominal values of the two coins were not the same.
    John Chown, citing Palgrave's dictionary, gives the following definition of Gresham's law:
    "Where by legal enactment a government assigns the same nominal value to two or more forms of circulatory medium whose intrinsic values differ, payment will always, as far as possible, be made in that medium of which the cost of production is least, and the more valuable medium will tend to disappear from circulation." Vide, Chown: *A History of Money, from AD 800.* London and New York: Routledge, 1996 : 17.
72. Tavernier put the value of *badam* at 35 to 40 almonds per *paisa,* while he found *cowrie* to be exchanged at 50 to 55 shells per *paisa.* Tavernier. *Travels in India,* Book 1, 22.
73. Deyell, John S. The Development of Akbar's Currency System.... 30.
74. For a description of the pluralistic monetary order in the immediate post-Plassey period, N.K. Sinha, *Economic History of Bengal,* Vol. I, Firma K.L. Mukhopadhyay, Kolkata: 1961, Ch. VIII, 129–156.
75. Ghoshal, Sarat Chandra. *A History of Coochbiher.* Siliguri : N.L. Publishers, 2005 : 27–28.
76. Prakash, Om. *The Dutch East India Company and the Economy of Bengal....* 232–34.

77. Vilar, Pierre. *A History of Gold and Money*, N.L.B., 1976, 50.
78. For a fairly detailed account, Om Prakash: Ibid, Chs. 5 & 6, 118–82.
79. Chaudhuri, K.N. *The Trading World of Asia and the English East India Company*, 1660–1760. C.U.P., 1978 : 153–158.
    Idem: "Towards an 'Intercontinental Model': Some Trends in Indo-European Trade in the Seventeenth Century". *I.E.S.H.R.* 6, no. 1 (1969) : 1–21.
80. We may, however, exclude Marx, in whose scheme demand entered through the crisis of realization.
81. Parker, Geoffrey. "The Emergence of Modern Finance in Europe 1500–1730" in *The Fontana Economic History of Europe*. Ed. C.M. Cipolla. *The Sixteenth and Seventeenth Centuries*. Glasgow: Collins/Fontana, 1974, 537–32.
    One excellent account of the production of counterfeit coins is to be found in John Styles. "Our traitorous Money Makers': The Yorkshire coiners and the law 1760–83. In *An UnGovernable People : The English and their law in the seventeenth and eighteenth centuries*. Ed. John Brewer and John Styles. London: Hutchinson, 1980.
82. Dasgupta, Ashin. "Indian merchants and the trade in the Indian Ocean, c1500–1750", *C.E.H.I.* 1, Ch. XII(2) : 426–35.
83. This is a well-noted event. Vide, Chandra, Satish. "Commercial Activities of the Mughal emperors during the Seventeenth Century". In *Essays in Medieval Indian Economic History*, Ed. Idem. Delhi : 1987 : 163–169. Prakash, Om. "The Indian Maritime Merchant, 1500–1800". *J.E.S.H.O.*, 47, no. 3 (2002) : 451.
    Subrahmanyam, Sanjay. "The Mughal State; Structure or Process—Reflections on Recent Western Historiography". *I.E.S.H.R.*, 29, no. 3 (1992): 315–16.
84. Bhadra, Gautam. *Mughal Juge Krishi Arthaniti....*, p. 108, Stephen Blake: *Shahjahanabad*, C.U.P., Indian edition, 1993 : 111.
    It is interesting that Blake, after conceding this point, comments that it was only under the English East India Company (itself a commercial power) that a true market economy hospitable to merchants began to develop. Ibid, 112.
85. Dasgupta, Ashin. "Indian Merchants and the Western Indian Oceans". *M.A.S.*, 19, no. 3 (1985) : 482–83.
86. Karen, Leonard. "The Great firm Theory of the Decline of the Mughal Empire". *C.S.S.H.* 21, no. 2 (1979). Reprinted in *The Mughal State.....* Eds.Alam and Subrahmanyam. 398–418.
    Richards, J.F. "Mughal State Finance and the Premodern World

Economy". *C.S.S.H.* 23, no. 3 (1981) : 285–308.

87. For a brief but elegant account, vide Bhadra, Gautam. *Mughal Juge Krishi Arthaniti....* Ch. 8, 125–210.
88. The concept of market-less trade was evolved by Karl Polanyi in order to describe situations where goods are exchanged, but prices are predetermined, not bargained.
89. Hicks, J.R. *Theory of Economic History.* Oxford: Clarendron Press, 1969 : 18–21.
90. Neale, Walter. "Reciprocity and Redistribution in the Indian Village: Sequel to Some Noble Discussions. In *Trade and Markets in Early Empires.* Eds. Polanyi, Arsenberg and Pearson. Illinois: Free Press and Falcon's Wing Press, 1957 : 227.
91. For a detailed treatment of the subject, vide Polanyi, Karl. *The Great Transformation—The Political and Economic Origins of Our Time.* Beacon Hill, Boston: Beacon Press, 1957 : particularly Chs. 4 & 5, 43–67. For a summary exposition, Polanyi: The Economy as Instituted Process... in *Trade and Markets in Early Empires,* 256–67.
92. For a reasonably good account, vide Sen: The Empire of Free Trade.... Ch. 1, 19–59.
93. For an elegant discussion of the subject, vide K.N. Chaudhuri: Markets and Traders in India .... 256–275.
94. Habib, Irfan. *The Agrarian System of Mughal India....,* Ch. 9. Muzaffar Alam: *The Crisis of Empire in Mughal North India" Awadh and Punjab,* 1707–1748. O.U.P., 1986 : passim.
    Bhadra, Gautam. *Muthal Juge Krishi Arthaniti....* Introduction
    Chandra, Satish. *Parties and Politics at the Mughal Court,* 1707–1740. Bengali Trl. C.P. Bandopadhya, K.P. Bagchi. Kolkata : 1978 : 36–43.
95. Ali, M. Athar. *The Mughal Nobility under Aurangzeb.* Bengali Trl. Arun Kumar De, K.P. Bagchi. Kolkata: 1978 : 36–43.
96. Misra, K.P. *Benaras in Transition.* Delhi : Manohar, 1975.
    "In eighteenth century upper India, while the basic currency unit of the Mughals, the *rupiya,* remained unaltered, a great change had taken place in purity and weight. This was the result of the adoption of a new system, that of farming out of mints introduced by Rattan Chand, diwan to Farrukhsiyar in about 1715. This practice, coupled with the decline of the imperial authority, led to the custom of debasing and charging the value of the coins, in some of the coins almost every year." Ibid, 176–177.
97. Habib, Irfan. Potentialities of Capitalist Development.... 232.

98. Dasgupta, Ashin. "Trade and Politics in Eighteenth Century India". In *The Mughal State* ..... Eds. Alam and Subrahmanyam. 370–80.
99. Bayly, C.A., *Rulers Townsmen and Bazaars: North Indian Society in the Age of British Expansion,* 1770–1879. C.U.P., 1983 : particularly the Introducion and Ch. 1, 1–73.
100. Gordon, Stewart. "The Slow Conquest: Administrative Integration of Malwa into the Maratha Empire". *M.A.S.* 11, no. 1 (1977): passim.
101. Grover. An Integrated Pattern of Commercial Life in the Rural Society of North India.... 249–50.
102. The history of the Jagat Seths is well-documented. Vide Little, J.H. *The House of Jagat Seth.* Calcutta Historical Society, 1960. For a brief account, vide Chaudhuri, Sushil. *From Prosperity to decline....* 109–116.
103. For a brief, but good account of the business operations of Khwaja Wazid and Omichand (Umichand), vide Chaudhuri, Sushil. Ibid.... 116–126.
104. Deyell, John S. Akbar's Currency System and Monetary Integration...., 45.
105. Perlin. *Unbroken Landscape.* Ashgate and Hampshire: Varorium, 1994 : 62–81.
106. Arthur Lewis's original and seminal article, "A model of Economic Development with Unlimited Supplies of labour", appeared in *Manchester School,* 1954. For an excellent critical interpretation, vide Mihir Rakshit's introduction to Sukhomoy Chakravarty's *Writings on Development,* O.U.P., 1997.

Chapter Three

Viewpoints on the Monetary System and Use of Money in the Pre-colonial South and the Deccan

Our discussion on the nature of commerce and use of money in Mughal India seems to have brought home some points. First of all, the picture of use of money gradually transcended the familiar image of a command economy, and mercantile wealth grew significantly over time. The crisis of the Mughal empire, however, cannot be attributed to the shift in the attitude of merchants and bankers. Rather, it would be more correct to say that big merchants and bankers, seeing the empire in a process of decay, shifted their allegiance, which in turn hastened the decline. Second, in the empire in general and in more commercialized regions like Bengal and Gujarat in particular, the volume and pattern of use of money discernibly outstripped the supply of imperial currencies.

Notwithstanding the system of free minting, the number and capacity of imperial mints were not sufficient to meet the demand for money. Even in a commercialized region like Bengal, there were periodic shortages of money and the rate of interest was high. The circulation of humble currency media like *cowrie* and *badam* cannot, however, be explained entirely by such dearth of supply of legal tender money. Here custom and tradition played their roles. The imperial state had to adjust to this tradition because the state of the economy was not strong enough to make such currency media redundant. Besides, the power of the imperial system of command was not uniform and what was possible in the core regions was not feasible in others. It may be suggested that the fact of circulation of such currency media constituted one of those aspects in terms of which the picture of the economy of Mughal India as a command economy needs to be qualified. Third, while the relation between extraction of surplus in the form of revenue-payment and use of money cannot be considered irrelevant, the promotion of the latter was determined by other factors as well. In places where there was significant growth of production in commercial crops, such as cotton and indigo, and where the manufacturing activities were predominantly rural, monetization definitely went beyond revenue payment.

On the nature of market formations, we have specified three categoris: standard and intermediate marketing centres, i.e. rural *haats* and *bazaars,* serving as foundational markets, urban consumer markets catering to the needs of the urban population and laslty, port markets located in India and abroad, acting as strategic points of entry of Indian goods into the international arena. We have also argued that although urbanization was a significant feature of Mughal India, the role of urban manufacturing in the Mughal economy was rather limited.

In studying the south Indian economy of the pre-colonial peroid, it should be noted at the outset that there are rival views on various aspects of the subject, and differences relate not only to points of emphasis, but to more fundamental issues like the nature of state formation as well. Burton Stein, in contrast to earlier interpretations, has emphatically advanced the idea of a segmentary state, in which effective state control was limited to a few core regions[1]; this view, taken in combination with the Aligarh view of the Mughal state structure, seems to suggest that the nature of state formation was fundamentally different between the Mughal north and the non-Mughal south. The difference between the two types of state formation, according to Sanjay Subrahamanyam, might not have been so great.[2] While it is not the objective or our study to examine the debate and judge the relative merits and demerits of the different approaches, we can suggest that as far as the nature of money use was concerned, it can be said that there was much in the

Mughal empire, at least in its more commercialized regions, which transcended the imperial monetary system. In this sense, one can draw a distinction between regions like Delhi and Agra and regions like Bengal and Gujarat, designating the former as core regions and the latter as non-core regions, because the imposition of the Mughal imperial monetary system was only partly effective in those two regions (or course, the *mansabdari* system does not by any means conform to the notion of a segmentary state). In Bengal, as we shall see, the *mansabdari* system was weak, and *zamindars* wielded much power. What we wish to hold is that in the light of recent research, Burton Stein's picture of state formation may be qualified to some extent, and that the Mughal state was not as much bureaucratic-patrimonial as it might first seem. According to the declared objective of our study, we may begin with the nature of the monetary system.

In south India, the objective basis of the circulation of a uniform King's money, however, evaporated with the decline and final collapse of the Vijaynagar empire, which had ruled a substantial part of the region for three centuries, in the early 18 century (whether we should call the Vijaynagar kingdom a segmentary state is another question) and the rise of successor states. After the decline of the kingdom, the character of the polity was definitely a confederate one. This character and, with the arrival of European companies, the setting up of a number of company mints allowed a multiplicity of currencies bearing the same name to circulate. The dominant currency in use was the *pagoda*, a gold coin of Vijaynagar descent. This 'strong' currency was produced by different mints operating under different authorities, including the Dutch and the English, and fetched different market values according to quality and popularity.[3] This suggests a pattern of coin production radically different from the Mughal norm, and this difference had something to do with the relatively decentralized nature of the polity. It may be said that in non-Mughal south, a good deal of merchants' money circulated in the name of King's money. Usually a *pagoda* had a value fluctuating around four silver rupees in the 17th-

18th centuries. During the reign of Tipu Sultan (1782-1799), one *pagoda* (*faruqi*) was the equivalent of three and half rupees in Mysore.[4] The coin next in the hierarchy was *fanam*, also termed *panam* or *fanas*. The humble currency media consisted of various copper coins, namely *kasu*, *doody* or *dubbu*, *nevel* and *paisa*. *Kasu* was a particularly low-value coin; one *fanam* was equivalent to more than 80 *kasus* and one *pagoda* equivalent to 16 to 18 *fanams*.[5] In short, *kasu* was a coin with a much lower value than the Mughal copper coin, although it was not as low-valued as *cowrie* of Bengal or even *badam* of Gujarat.

The expansion of the Mughal empire southwards led to the production of Mughal *rupayaas* in Golconda mints, and Europeans began to coin *Arcot* and Madras rupees in the second half of the 17th century. The latter were, however, meant primarily for trade with Surat, north India and Bengal.[6]

The evolution of the *fanam* in the 17th century is interesting, and acquires special significance in the light of the possible impact of massive influx of silver into India in the 17th century on the monetary system. Although the impact of this influx in the north Indian context have been discussed at length by the Aligarh historians, such a discussion is sadly missing in the historiography of south India. It cannot be said that the influx of New World silver into the Indian subcontinent produced no effect on the south Indian economy. In Sanjay Subrahmanyam's fairly detailed study of south Indian Commerce (1550-1650), it is categorically mentioned that silver as a currency metal was alien to south India during this period, and the *fanam* was a gold coin with a copper alloy.[7] Again, Sinnappa Arsaratnam's study of Coromandel commerce of the later period (1650-1740) suggests the *fanam* to be a mixed coin of gold and silver.[8] These two apparently contradictory pieces of information indicate that the metallic contents of the *fanam* underwent an evolution under the impact of the influx of silver. Taken in conjunction with the low-value copper coins, it can be said that since the mid-17th century, the Coromandel region witnessed some sort of a system of trimetallism, with the difference that the circulation of *pagodas* and half-*pagodas* remained dominant. But silver as a currency metal grew in importance, as is evidenced by the production of silver *fanams* by the Europeans in Madras (now Chennai) and Pondicherry.[9] While there can be no gainsaying that the position of silver as a currency metal in the south was not in the same bracket, not even in the same street, as that in contemporary north, it is curious that about the middle of the 17th century, the gold–silver price ratio in Masulipatnam, the premier port town of the north Coromandel region, was substantially higher than that in Surat. In the 1640s it was 17.2 to 17.5:1 at Masulipatnam, while at Surat, it was 14.2 to 14.3:1.[10] This anomaly is even more puzzling considering the well-noted historical fact that foreigners had traditionally been bringing gold into the Coromandel region. One possible explanation might be that gold was in high demand for coinage and other purposes, including gifts and ornament making, which maintained the relative price of gold at a higher level. Surat was the premier entrepot for the inflow of silver into the Indian subcontinent. But the demand for silver for coinage was particularly acute there, especially in view of the fact that large quantities of silver regularly flew from Surat to upper India in the form of rupee coins, and also because during this period, there was a general shortage of copper for coinage. Yet the regional difference in the ration of gold to silver prices leaves some other points to be explained. The data collected by Irfan Habib show that in Mughal India as a whole, the highest value of gold-silver price ration was 16.4 :1 in 1658—assuming that gold in a *muhr* and silver in a rupee were practically of equal weight[11]—which is less than Subrahmanyam's figure (17.2) for Masulipatnam in the 1640s. It is also interesting that despite huge imports of gold,[12] the gold–silver price ratio did not show any tendency of equalization threreafter. This is corroborated by Arasaratnam's findings, suggesting that the *pagoda*-rupee exchange ratio remained fairly stable in the second half of the 17th and the first decades of the 18th century. Arasaratnam's own words summarizing his findings may be quoted here: "The exchange rate between the rupee and the *pagoda* was reasonably stable during this period, the *pagoda* tending marginally to fall relative to the rupee as the rupee became more current, at least in European overseas trade. .... In the mid-17th century the *pagoda* fetched about 3 rupees. In the early 18th century the French fixed the exchange rate at Rs 320 for 100 pagodes, but merchants were demanding Rs 370 or 380, reflecting the demand for pagodas relative to rupees. In the 1730s the pagoda was exchanging on the Coromandel Coast for Rs 3. The exchange rate fluctuated within a range of 6 per cent."[13] Of course, it is difficult to suggest that the specific monetary conditions of Surat are applicable to the whole of Mughal India. Can it be argued that in the Coromandel region the demand for gold for coinage and other purposes was too high? This is not too absurd an argument. But what is not so easily understandable is why, in spite of the much discussed massive inflow of silver, the gold–silver price ratio in Mughal India should have remained lower than that in the Coromandel region. We cannot provide a satisfactory answer to this question unless much more evidence regarding the demand conditions of these two metals is brought to light. What we can suggest is that in explaining the relative importance of flow of different metals, as well as non-metallic currency media, the old supply-centric approach should be qualified, if not rejected. Another question concerns the extent of inter-regional flow of precious metals. If a significant difference persisted over a long stretch of time, it only follows that the inter-regional integration was not very strong. High gold prices in the Coromandel region ostensibly attracted foreign merchants, but not those domestic traders of Mughal India, who dealt in gold and silver.

Frank Perlin has drawn attention to the cheapness of production of *pagodas* relative to the *muhrs* turned out by the Mughal mints. Here it should be emphasized that without the demand for use of gold coins, a demand largely rooted in the tradition of south India, simplified technology would not constitute a proper explanation for the circulation of *pagodas* as the dominant coin.[14] The major difficulty in accepting Perlin's suggestion is that there is no reason why the logic of simpler technology and reduced cost of production should not have been applicable to silver coins as well. Of course, it is difficult to pronounce a judgment on this issue without adequate information on the output of *pagodas* over different time periods.

We may now venture a few words about price movements. On this topic, there is much less study regarding south India than the Mughal north or Bengal. We can nevertheless try to form an opinion from the standard studies. It seems that prices of copper in the north Coromandel region rose somewhat in the 1640s, after remaining stationary in the earlier decades of the 17th century, and the price of rice was stable, measured in gold or copper.[15] These findings differ somewhat with those of Arasaratnam, according to whom, "There was a steady increase in the price of rice from the beginning of the 17th century throughout the empire."[16] The latter also suggests that the price rise since the 1690s was steep and fluctuating.[17] Of course, Arasaratnam's evidence is very fragmentary and unsystematic, and it is difficult to draw any definite conclusion from it.

Let us now examine the nature of market formations. apart from large port markets, two other types are found, *petais* (town markets) and *santas* (periodic rural markets). One scholar notes, "Coarse cloth for local consumption was produced virtually everywhere and the cloth was sold at weekly fairs called *santa*, the north Indian equivalent being the *haat*."[18] How far such a comparison between the *haat* and the *santa* is really apposite may be a meaningful question to ask. As we have noted, *haats* and more regular rural markets like country *bazaars* played the role of foundational markets in Mughal India. It is in these *haats* and *bazaars* that the tie between revenue and trade was formed, and consumption goods started their movements towards towns and cities. In south India, on the other hand, this role of *haats* was largely absent owing to the large-scale presence of coastal commerce, which supplied in large measure the consumption needs of towns and in some cases of the interior as well. This role was more pronounced in the case of rice, which was the staple food grain of south India. Evidence of large-scale imports of rice from eastern India in order to feed the population of Masulipatnam is found for the late 16th century. In the 17th century, this role of coastal trade continued as well. According to Subrahamanyam, a part of this rice went to feed the weaving population of the Krishna delta.[19] From Arasaratnam's study, we learn that from the second decade of the 18th century, there were large and regular imports of rice from Bengal to Madras and the neighbouring port of San Thome, and the imported rice was carried to various administrative centres. The servants of the English Comapny and European free merchants also participated in this trade.[20] To sum up, we find that in meeting the needs of the urban population of south India, coastal commerce had a prominent role. It is this role of coastal commerce that suggests a basic difference as between the north and the south. What we find in south India is a disjuncture between commerce in the interior and that in the cities.

We have already argued that some sort of a system of trimetallism in south India came into being in the 17th-18th centuries in the wake of the general spurt in the inflow of silver into the Indian subcontinent. However, there were some basic differences of this system with its counterpart in Mughal India, which may be summarized as follows: First, coins bearing the same name, but produced at different mints were not uniform in terms of weight and finesse in the south. Second, the dominant currency metal was gold, not silver and this dominance had more to do with demand than with supply. Third, mixed gold and silver coins were alien to Mughal India, but not to the south.

A few lines, although somewhat speculative, may be ventured on the respective areas of circulation of *pagodas, fanams* and copper coins. Pagodas and half-*pagodas* were presumably exchanged in relatively high-valued and bulk transactions, e.g. those between companies and big merchants, and among merchants themselves. Smaller transactions were conducted in *fanams* and copper coins. Miniscule transactions at *santas* and *petais* were possibly dominated by copper coins such as *kasu*. It is worth noting that this particular coin had a number of types and each type circulated in a specific locality.[21]

We may now try to consider the applicability or otherwise of the view of a direct functional relation between revenue payment and marketing of produce in the context of south India. In the context of Mughal India, such a view might have some justification at least, although the Aligarh historians' interpretation of it possibly bears the mark of some sort of overemphasis. The available studies on south Indian commerce do not lend credence to such a view. Sanjay Subrahmanyam observes, "Curiously enough, both the areas on the southern Indian coastline that participated in the export of rice in considerable degrees were areas where land was extensively held by privileged groups, either lightly taxed and somewhat papered Brahmin communities, or influential institutions, temples, mathas and the like."[22] This suggestion of the absence of a strong positive correlation between monetization and tax-payment may be corroborated by the available information on the development of the textile economy. The growth of specialized weaving villages—for example, Virana villages of the second half of the 17th century—producing textiles for exports and located strategically near the ports is well-attested.[23] When large numbers of direct producers specializing in a single product were settled in clusters of villages and produced almost entirely for distant markets, it was quite natural for them to depend for their victual and other necessities on nearby market places. In the dry upland frontier regions, land was given to local soldiers and land revenue was low. In such areas, local chiefs used to combine tax collection, agriculatural trading, long distance shipping and banking operations.[24] If land revenue was low, but trading, banking and shipping activities were prominant, the need for revenue payment could not be the determining factor of monetization. Sanjay Subrahmanyam's intensive study of the commercial economy of the north Coromandel economy in the late 17th century has also highlighted the importance of coastal trade as well as short-distance movements in the transporatation of rice. He has argued that the growth of rural industry, particularly textiles, was accompanied by a concurrent growth of commercial agriculture. Of course, he has also stressed the importance of imported goods, not only of rice, but of cotton also, in sustaining the industry. The thrust of his argument is that the growth of commercialization led to a high degree of spatial differentiation.[25] This view is corroborated by Joseph Brennig's findings on the transfer of huge quantities of raw cotton from the Deccan coast to the northern Coromandel region.[26] Such studies establish that south India, particularly south-eastern India, witnessed a situation in which monetization must have been considerable, and it is difficult to correlate the degree of monetization with the imperatives of revenue payment.

Compared with the Mughal north, this suggests some sort of a difference, even if we do not uncritically accept the emphasis of Habib on the direct relation between surplus extraction and monetization. This difference is possibly explicable, at least partially, on the impetus provided by export trade. Demands for textiles and consequent spatial specialization should promote use of money for meeting the daily necessities and raw materials of manufacture, not for revenue payment alone.

Turning to what is known as the Maratha region, we find a picture that is at the same time similar to and different from that found in the Coromandel region. Coastal and overseas commerce were not sources of acquisition of wealth (periodic plunder of Surat notwithstanding). This is one important distinction. Yet the scale of money use was substantial and growing, and there were many different coin-types in circulation. Frank Perlin's somewhat detailed study has thrown interesting light on the scale and mode of money use in western Deccan. He suggests a growing process of monetization of the agrarian economy in the 17th century and the establishment of a generalized culture of money use even among poor peasants and artisans in the 18th.[27] In the expanding Maratha empire, the emphasis on regular armies needed salary payments in cash and settlements were also made in cash. Stewart Gordon describes the promotion of monetization in the Maratha region in the 18th century excellently in the following words, "Several developments in the eighteenth century made traders very important to the Marathas. Maratha forces had shifted from roving bands to large, mercenary armies. At the opening of the century, Maratha troops were lightly armed, highly mobile, and recruited mainly with the promise of booty. ...By mid-century, there were permanent camps of 50000 men and more, each soldier needing salary. This pressure for cash to pay the troops generated an increasing monetization throughout the countryside. In Malwa and Khandesh, there were virtually no settlements in kind by mid-century. With land taxes collected in cash, traders were the means by which cash reached the countryside. In the few Maratha records that list the actual production of a village, what is surprising is the variety of cash crops that are grown in addition to basic grains and dals."[28] The process of integration of the Mughal province of Malwa into the Maratha kingdom and the administration of the province, as described by Gordon in another paper, suggests that the Marathas, after capturing this province, erected an apparatus of revenue collection that was well-directed and supervised by civilians named *kamavisdars,* an apparatus that was "the exact antithesis of the marauding raids of the previous two decades", i.e. the 1720s and 1730s. Gordon also suggests that the collection of revenue under the Marathas was at first low, but then it increased and in 1755-57, it was not much lower than what was under the Mughals in 1700. Gordon also informs us that new towns grew up and flourished while those that had prospered under the Mughals decayed.[29] In short, it is clear that the Maratha rulers set up over time a well-arranged system of revenue collection, and monetization proceeded as a necessary concomitant of it. This ostensibly required minting activities. Another factor propelling the spread of minting activities was the policy of expansion and hegemony in the 18th century. As one distinguished student of the late pre-colonial Maratha economy has put it succinctly, "In the 18th century, the Marathas, who had adopted a policy of expansion in the north and hegemony in the south... involved themselves in continuous wars. Consequently their demands for financing military operations and keeping the conquered territories under control increased beyond their expectations. This led to the establishment of more mints and the emergence of a new class of *sahukars* (moneylenders) who could meet the growing requirements of the state."[30] One of them, the Dixit-Pattabardhans, became the bankers of the Peshwas and had branches in every important town of the Maratha region. The operation of this banking house transcended the boundary of functioning of traditional indigenous *sahukars*.[31]

Perlin in his research has tried to relate the number of mints with expansion in use of money. Members of the military/ politial elite and merchants/bankers set up mints, not only in important cities like Pune and Kohlapur, but in small towns and country markets as well. According to Perlin's account, the coins turned out by these mints can be classified into two general types. At the mints set up by the ruling authorities, such as the Pune regime or the Sindhes, usually good quality coins were produced. These authorities were concerned with monetary transactions over wider areas and wanted to have reliable sources of cash at hand. The other type consisted of low quality coins produced in massive quantities at mints controlled by local merchants. Perlin has named these media 'gimcrack coins'. He suggests that coin production spread to the village level also.[32] This suggestion is supported by John Malcom's evidence on the minting system in central India ruled by the Sindhes in the early 19th century. "The coinage of Ojein, Indore and Bhopal, has maintained a sufficient degree of credit and purity, while that of Pertapgarh not only varies continually, but has generally been increasing its quantity of alloy from twenty five to twenty six grains each rupee... The principles and processes of coining are nearly the same in all the mints of Central India, except at Pertapgarh, where the monopoly is vested in four mercantile houses."[33] This evidence shows that merchants minted coints to be used in localized spheres of exchanges, i.e. 'captive' coin markets. The same evidence of multiplicity of coins is found from the regions later coming under the Bombay Presidency. In the early 18th century, the British conquerors found at least 38 kinds of gold and 127 kinds of silver coins circulating there, besides copper and *cowrie*.[34] A.R. Kulkarni has listed 55 types of silver coins—the list is not, however, exhaustive—in circulation in the Maratha region in the 18th century.[35] It may be noted here that merchants' money, i.e. the monetary media produced by merchants, circulated locally or regionally; but they were unable to compete with what, following Hicks, may be called King's money. Yet there can be no gainsaying that there was growing and widespread use of money.

This phenomenon of localized circulation of money requires careful treatment. Some degree of localism is inevitable in a pre-modern market, where metallic money, rather than paper money as the debt obligation of the state, is the common medium of exchange. Even in a relatively modern market, some degree of localism might appear when the issues made by the centralized authorities are inadequate for meeting the needs of exchange, as was evidenced by the circulation of the notes and tokens issued by country bankers during the Industrial Revolution in Britain.[36] The Mughal regions with their centralized system of minting were also not free from it. For example, a *sicca* rupee coined in Patna lost in exchange value when it reached Hooghly, where Murshidabad rupees were more popular.[37] This is one point. The second point worthy of attention is that coins lacking in uniformity and popularity were used locally by merchants who themselves were engaged in large-scale trading (we may note Malcom's reference to mercantile houses). The merchants produced these coins in order to make payments to peasants and artisans who did not need good quality coins for day-to-day transactions. So, despite the lack of uniformity and quality, these coins served to link remote producing areas with nearby and distant town markets.

One may argue by referring to *cowrie*-using Bengal that money-use in this region was more reflective of economic integration than the Deccan and the South, as *cowrie* was uniformly used in low value exchanges. As against this, it can be reasonably held that *cowrie* could not be fabricated, and so, the question of production of high or low-quality *cowries* could not arise. More important the prices of *cowrie* in terms of silver rupees were not the same everywhere. Rather, it might be said that the role played by low-priced and crude copper coins, produced by gimcrack techniques in the Maratha regions was analogous with that performed by *cowrie* in Bengal. *Cowrie* was also a currency medium that served to link the cloth and rice-producing villages of Bengal with far distant markets.

Our analysis of the monetary order of pre-colonial India highlights one point : the centralized Mughal system of minting of standardized coins is too inadequate a framework for understanding the nature of use of money. Not only non-Mughal, but non-imperial and non-royal currencies too had their roles as well. The Mughal system, with its emphasis on uniformity should be viewed as a part of the overall pattern of money use. We should pay more attention to the non-imperial and humble currency media if our understanding of the nature and scale of use of money in pre-colonial India is to be deepened.

We have already referred to the well-known fact that the monetary system of pre-colonial India was heavily dependent on imports of metals, such as gold, silver, copper, etc. and nonmetallic currency media like *cowrie* and *badam*. This was true for the north and south alike. The possible impact of this commodity composition of imports on the economy in terms of output and employment is a subject meriting an analytical examination. The subject has been approached from different angles and controversies have arisen. We have already pointed out the difficulties of proving the hypothesis of the 'price revolution', but this does not in any way negate the necessity of examining the possible impact of this inflow in terms of other macroeconomic variables.

We now propose to put forward the different opinions in a nutshell and then offer our own. Let us start in all fairness with Professor K.N. Chaudhuri, whose work on Company trading has rightfully commanded a great deal of respect. K.N. Chaudhuri, in his celebrated book, *The Trading World of Asia and the English East India Company,* has commented, "The huge influx of bullion which resulted from the new demand was only an indication of the growth of income and employment. The export of textiles turned the coastal provinces of India into major industrial towns, and the bullion imported by the Companies passed directly into circulation as payments for export goods."[38] It should be noted that this link between growth of income and employment and influx of bullion needs to be analyzed in a cause-effect manner. As income grows, imports, bullion or no bullion, should also grow as a function of income. In this sense, Professor Chaudhuri's remark contains some truth—because income and employment had risen, the economy was importing huge amounts of bullion and specie because of its enhanced capability to absorb them. Here the increased import of bullion and specic is a consequence, not a cause, of increased income. Now, the impact of increased expots on the level of income and employment should be very positive if there are unemployed resources, because the Keynesian multiplier should then work, if factor constraints are not binding. If such resources do exist in sufficient quantities, there is little possibility of inflation, because the initial inflationary pressure is likely to be burned out by output adjustment. But we should also keep in mind that Keynes built his theoretical framework on essentially short-run considerations in which the economy operates at less than full employment level and there is no serious problem of inter-sectoral imbalances. In the long run, the impact of exports might not be as strong if the country exporting manufactures cannot ensure an adequate supply of those goods that enter into the manufacturing process, directly and indirectly. These goods are invariably capital goods and wage goods. Without the import of such goods, the monetized sector might expand if the imported objects help in the promotion of monetization in the economy, drawing increasing areas and increasing quantities of goods into the nexus of money use, and here increased exports play a definite role in so far as it boosts the demand. But this does not imply a sustained growth of real income over an entire historical epoch. With growth of population, and a favourable land–man ratio, more land, however, may be brought under cultivation and more tools for the production of industrial consumer goods may be produced in the long run.

Here it can be pointed out that Indian merchants' sale of Indian goods to European companies and other merchants used to take place in a number of ways. Indian merchants either acted as intermediaries on behalf of European companies and Asian merchants in the matter of procurement or sold their procured goods directly to foreign merchants at ports lying in India and abroad. Besides, there was overland trade. But all constituted parts of India's foreign trade, bringing in precous and non-precious metals, non-metallic monetary substances, and items like good-quality horses. This export-import process allowed mercantile wealth to reproduce and expand itself. Continuous additions to the domestic stocks of gold, silver, copper, *cowrie,* etc. must have added to the wealth of merchants who could appropriate increasing shares of this stock through this process. This point can be appreciated if it is kept in mind that merchants grew in importance in pre-colonial India over time. Internal trade allowed merchants to appropriate a share of the domestic surplus of physical goods such as textiles, raw silk, rice by investing their money. But this money wealth of the mercantile class as a whole could not grow unless they could sell these commodities to foreigners. Additions to stocks of precious metals by way of imports, in this sense, can be treated as an index of growth of mercantile wealth (we should, however, be charry of confusing money with wealth). Such additions, however, cannot by themselves boost real income and output in the long run, unless they are used for importing wage goods or capital equipments. This wealth did not pass solely to export merchants and was shared in varying degrees by all sections of the trading hierarchy, because export goods had to pass through the hands of a series of intermediaries before reaching the ports.

With this observation in the background, we can examine two approaches to the subject just mentioned. One view, developed in terms of an analytically rigorous model by Professor Mihir Rakshit, is that the volume of international trade can boost economic activity in a backward, predominantly agrarian economy only in so far as it propels the surplus-consuming sterile classes to have more precious metals and thus to release more marketable surplus of agricultural consumption goods for the mainenance of a large number of workers in the non-manufacturing sector.[39] Such a model might be considered apposite when precious metals and other forms of commodity money are regarded only as wealth of the sterile classes (here the Mughal and non-Mughal ruling classes, and other classes directly appropriating surplus), i.e. when the demand for precious metals is either for hoarding or for satisfying something like the 'oriental penchant for ornaments', and merchants are considered as playing only a subsidiary role and having no room for accumulation. To the extent that the so-called 'oriental penchant for ornaments' and 'the propensity to hoard' worked, this model has some utility in explaining the impact of the inflow of precious metals on the Indian economy. But if we assume that the demand for currency media was a great propelling factor in the imports of precious metals and also non-metallic substances like *cowrie* and *badam*—such an assumption is not unreasonable—we have to consider the role of merchants and here the model loses its usefulness. Another opinion, a typically Keynesian one, is that the growing demand for India's exportable goods increased income and employment. In this view, the direct impact of precious metal flows is not considered, and what is stressed is the level of injection, in the sense of traditional national income accounting, into the economy in the form of export demands from abroad. This view, put forward by Professor Om Prakash and concurred with by Professor Sushil Chaudhuri in the context of Bengal, might be agreeable if there is no evidence of any inflationary price trend and if there is supposed to exist some unemployed resources in the economy, which could be more fully utilized in response to increased external demand.[40] This view should be scrutinized carefully. Suppose textile spinners and weavers now get more work and demand more wage goods. Of course, food grains constitute the major portion of wage goods. In this case, the output of food grains can rise only if there are unutilized labour and land. Land might be abundant, but the availability of labour is slow to increase, and hence increase in the supply of wage goods is not to be achieved quickly in the absence of discernible technological progress in agriculture. Yet it is perhaps a better hypothesis than the earlier physiocratic notion. But here too, no independent attention is given to the growing monetization, and no role is assigned to merchants and no explanation is advanced as to why Indian merchants should import large quantities of gold, silver, copper, *cowrie*, etc. Our point is that with the growth of commercialization and growing monetization, the demand for money grew, necessitating such imports. It is wrong to attribute the demand for precious metals solely or even predominantly to the so-called 'oriental perchant for ornaments' and the hoarding habits of the people. Hoarding might have been a feature of the economic life of the people, but it was not of such an order that the flow of money would be impaired. On the other hand, the merchants as a whole appropriated an increasing volume of surplus through internal trade, and converted this surplus into money form through external trade. This autonomous accumulation of mercantile wealth has in general been neglected in the discussions on the subject.[41] Is may be pointed out that although the hypothesis of the price revolution remains unproven, accumulation of mercantile wealth does not depend on such phenomena; what is necessary is a general expansion of commercial activites. That this took place is pre-colonial India over time is an incontestable historical fact.

This point can be further extended. While India, in the 17th-18th centuries, was using imported monetary media for her internal exchange needs, paper money was increasingly making its presence felt in Europe, replacing gold and silver, and they were at least partly independent of actual coinage. As Braudel and Spooner, in their classic survey, have observed on the use of fiduciary and fiat money in Europe, "By the seventeenth century, its presence was already insistent, as the indispensable concomitant of gold and silver, those two great actors, so to speak, prevented from playing their full parts. This was on the eve of triumph in the eighteenth century. Whatever its nature, paper money was based upon the money of account. The first bank notes merely gave it material form.[42] Pre-colonial India witnessed the growth of large banking firms having close liaison with regional state powers, such as the Jagat Seths, Dixit-Pattabardhans, etc.[43] and a flourishing business in *hundis* (promissory notes and bills of exchange). But these *hundis* were not replacements of metallic currencies, as they were not always usable either for accouting purposes or as stores of value. Only a part of the hundis, i.e., those that did not have any time dimension and hence were saleable at a discount could be treated partially as money, but they were not comparable with the notes issued by the Bank of England. Those notes were backed by gold and silver, but with the growth of the credibility of the bank. The need for conversion of these notes diminished progressively. It might be that the abundance of gold, silver and copper in India prevented the rise of such institutions. The bills of exchange in India were not synonymous with fiat money. The creation of book money without use of cash was of a very limited nature and there was no centralized institution with enough credibility to give them popular backing. In Europe, the increased use of fiat money was caused by the expansion of the monetization in the internal economies, large outflows of precius metals owing to the compulsions of trade with the Orient and the rise to power of the new commercial bourgeoisie and the new landed moneyocracy.[44] The increased demand for money for internal exchange was met not by metallic currency but by fiat money. The relative centralization achieved in Britain made it possible for the conversion of gold and silver into stocks and use them for exports, and to that extent, her economy benefited. In pre-colonail India, the accumulation of stocks might have augumented the wealth of merchants. It is perhaps possible to analyze the dynamics of the economy is a somewhat better way by examining the interaction of the state, surplus creating direct producers and merchants.

In our earlier discussion (vide Chapter 2) we have rejected the atrophy thesis. But this rejection leads to other sorts of questions. One might feel tempted to call what developed in India as some sort of proto-capitalism. This view has some apparent justification at least in view of the recent research on the intensity of circulation of money at different levels. The question is how and why this development came to a halt. The English Company's triumphant entry into the politics of the Indian subcontinent and their expansionary activities might be called the reason. But the question that goes abegging is how such a permanent trimph, as distinguished from temporary acts of plunder, did occur. Is it explicable in terms of superior military might alone?

West European feudalism was possibly a weaker economic formation that broke down under the impact of its own rapidly maturing internal contradictions, and its dissolution was hastened by the growth of commerce. In pre-colonial India, there were large peasant revolts as well as sizeable accumulation of mercantile wealth. But this growth of commerce and money use did not have the same parametric effect as in Western Europe. Indian mercantile wealth had ultimately to capitulate to Europeans and those who fought ultimately perished, although they did not always give up their ground so easily. Is the weakness displayed by Indian mercantile wealth explicable in terms of some sort of procurement base or investment crisis that finally drove them to Europeans or force them to wind up their independent functioning? If in Europe, gold and silver could play a positive role by boosting mercantile profits, much of which was recycled into industry, what prevented such inflows from playing a similar role in India? A conclusive and fairly acceptable answer is yet to be found, unfortunately though.

NOTES AND REFERENCES

1. For a brief, but clear presentation of Stein's views, vide Stein. "The State and the Economy, The South". *C.E.H.I.*, I, Ch. VII(3) : 205–08. His views are presented more elaborately in Stein: *Vijayanagar, The New Cambridge History of India*, 1.2, Orient Longman, 1988 : Chs. 3&4, passim.
2. Subrahmanyam, Sanjay. *The Political Economy of Commerce in South India* 1550–1650. C.U.P., 1990 : 39–45.
3. Arasaratnam, S. *Merchants, Companies and Commerce on the Coromandel Coast* 1650–1730. O.U.P., 1986 : 295–304.
4. Hasan, Mohibbul. *History of Tipu Sultan*. Reprint. Delhi : Aakar Books, 2006 : Appendix C, 397.
5. Arasaratnam, S. op. cit. 306, 320.
6. Ibid : 307–312.
7. Subrahmanyam, Sanjay. *The Political Economy of Commerce....*, 370–72.
8. Arasaratnam, S. op.cit., 305–307.
9. Ibid, 306–07.
10. Subrahmanyam, Sanjay. op. cit. 82–85.
11. Habib, Irfan. A System of Trimetallism in the Age of the Price Revolution........... Table 2.
12. Subrahmanyam, Sanjay. *The Political Economy of Commerce .....*, 84, Arasaratnam : *Merchants, Companies and Commerce....* 286–97, 300–301.

13. Arasaratnam. Ibid, 319–20.
14. Perlin, Frank. "Money Use in Late Precolonial India and International Trade in Currency Media". *The Imperial Monetary System of Mughal India.* Ed. J.F. Richard. O.U.P., 1987 : 251–52.
15. Subrahmanyam, Sanjay. *The Political Economy of Commerce in South India,* pp. 350–51, Table 7.1, also Idem: Precious Metal Flows and Prices..., Idem (ed.): *Money and Market in India* 1100–1700. O.U.P. 1994 : 206–207.
16. Arasaratnam. Ibid, 337.
17. Ibid, 335–338.
18. Ramaswami, Vijaya. *Textiles and Weavers in Medieval South India,* O.U.P. 1985, 128.
19. Subrahmanyam : Rural Industry and Commercial Agriculture in Late Seventeenth Century South Eastern India, *Past and Present,* (Feb. 1990) : 103–104.
20. Arasaratnam. *"The Rice Trade in Eastern India 1650–1740" M.A.S.* 22, no. 3 (1988) : 543–44.
21. Idem : Merchants, Companies and Commerce..... 320.
22. Subrahmanyam, S. *The Political Economy of Commerce in South India....* 66.
23. For a general discussion on the weaving villages, Arasaratnam. Ch. 2, passim. Kasi Virana was the chief merchant of the English East India Company in the Southern Coromandel region during 1660–1680. An account of his relation with the Company is to be found in Joseph Brennig. "Chief Merchants and European, Enclaves in Seventeenth Century Coromandel." *M.A.S.* II, no. 3 (1977) : 333–338.
24. Stein, Burton. *Vijaynagar : The New Cambridge History of India.* 1.2. Orient Longman, 1988 : 128–29.
25. Subrahmanyam, S. "Rural Industry and Commercial Agriculture in South Eastern India" *Past and Present.* (February 1990) : 76–114, passim.
26. Brennig, Joseph. "Textile Producers and Production in Late Seventeenth Century Coromandel". In *Markets Merchants and State in Early Modern India.* O.U.P., 1990 : 68–69.
27. Perlin, Frank. *Money Use in late Precolonial India and International Trade in Currency Media.* 256–277.
28. Gordon, Stewart. "Burhanpur: Entrepot and Hinterland". *I.E.S.H.R.,* 25, no. 4 (1988) : 440.
29. Idem "The Slow Conquest: Administrative Integration of Malwa into the Maratha Empire" *M.A.S.* 11, no. 1 (1977) : 31–38.
30. Kulkarni, A.R. "Money and Credit under the Marathas,

Seventeenth century to AD 1848". In *Money and Credit in Indian History from the Early Medieval Times.* Ed. Amiya Bagchi. Delhi : Tulika, 2002, 94.

31. Kulkarni, "G.T. Banking in the Eighteenth Century; The Case Study of a Pune Banker". *Artha-Vijjana.* (June 1973) : 180–200, passim.
32. Perlin, Frank. Money Use in Late Precolonial India...., 299–300. For further information, Perlin. "Mint Technology and Mint Output in an Age of Growing Commercialization". In *Essays in Mediaeval Indian Economic History.* Ed. Satish Chandra. Delhi : Munshiram Manoharlal, 1987 : 292–303.
33. Malcom, John. *A Memoir of Central India,* Vol. II. Reprint. Delhi : Sagar Publications, 1970 : 80–85.
34. Fukazawa, H. "The State and Economy—Maharastra and the Deccan". *C.E.H.I.,* 1, : 202.
35. Kulkarni, A.R. Money and Credit Under the Marathas...., 103–04.
36. In L.S. Pressnell's book on country banks, the author remarks that these country bankers, "would have been of smaller importance if the mint and eighteenth century government had met their responsibilities for providing the country with an adequate currency". Pressnell. *Country Banking in the Industrial Revolution.* Oxford : Clarendron Press, 1956 : 14.
37. Chaudhuri, K.N. *The Trading World of Asia and the English East India Company.* C.U.P., 1978 : 183.
38. Chaudhuri, K.N. *The Trading World of Asia and the English East India Company.* C.U.P., 1978 : 183.
39. Rakshit, Mihir Kanti. *The Labour Surplus Economy: A Neo-Keynesian Approach.* India: Macmillan, 1982 : 48–55.
40. Prakash, Om. "Bullion for Goods; International Trade and the Economy of Early Eighteenth Century Bengal". *I.E.S.H.R.* 13, no. 2 (1976) : 159–87, passim.
    Chaudhuri, Sushil. *From Prosperity to Decline : Bengal in the Eighteenth Century....* 304–05.
41. Here we wish to draw attention to one relatively unnoticed work in which this point has been discussed. vide Majumdar, Arun. *Structural Evolution of the Indian Economy, Early Phase.* Delhi : Mahohar, 1992 : Chs. 4.2 & 4.3, 195–223, passim.
42. Braudel and Spooner. "Prices in Europe from 1450 to 1750". In *Cambridge Economic History of Europe.* Vol. IV. Eds. E.E. Rich and C.H. Wilson. Cambridge, 1967 : 380.
43. For Dixit-Pattabardhans, G.T. Kulkarni: *Banking in the Eighteenth*

Century....; For the Jagat Seths, vide Chapter 5 of this book and other references given in the footnotes to Chapter 2.

44. Karl Marx trenchantly summed up the character of the new land-owning class in this worlds: "The old nobility had been devoured by the great feudal wars. The new nobility was the child of its time, for which money was the power of all powers." *Das Capital*, Vol. 1. Moscow, 1986 : 672.

Chapter Four

An Overview of the Pre-Colonial Bengal Economy

This is a discussion on the monetary transition in Bengal as a specific case study. This choice obviously requires an explanation. It should be noted that Bengal was incorporated into the Mughal empire in the process of their imperial conquest, but the Mughal revenue administration, notwithstanding the detailed assessments, could not be entirely effective, nor could the imperial nonetary system be imposed in totality. Bengal was formally a Mughal *subah* (province) ever since its annexation by Emperor Akbar in 1576, but a considerable part of the province remained under the Afghan chiefs who defied the authority of the Mughals. In 1612, the last of these chiefs was defeated. The final Mughal annexation, however, had to wait till 1666 when Shaista Khan, the then governor of the province, wrested Chittagong, a centre of maritime trade, from Portuguese occupation.[1] Another significant fact was that the geography of Mughal Bengal was considerably different from that of colonial Bengal. The districts of Bhagalpur, Purnea and Syllet were within Mughal Bengal. They were ceded during the British period.

John S. Deyell has correctly noted that "the *Ain-i-Akbari II* gives a more thorough analysis of the administrative divisions of Bengal than any other suba."[2] But he has failed to note the unreliability of the statistics therein.

Five of the nineteen *sarkars* (districts) mentioned in the *Ain-i-Akbari,* namely Bakla, Chatgaon (Chittagong), Sonargaon, Fatehabad and Sylhat (Syllet), were then outside the control of the Mughals. It is highly probable that the revenue assessments of these areas were dependent on the records maintained by the earlier Sultani government.[3] This was definitely at variance with the standard Mughal practice of collecting information on cultivated area, yield and prices. The assessed figures for Bengal were supplemented by cesses. The original valuation was revised subsequently from time to time.

An error in the *Ain-i-Akbari*, unnoticed by James Grant as well as by later historians but pointed out by Irfan Habib, should be mentioned. In the *Ain*, the combined assessment for Bengal and Orissa is shown to be 598459319 copper *dams*, in which Bengal's share was 42,51 03200 *dams*. Irfan Habib has pointed out that the *jama* for Orissa was counted twice over. According to Habib's revised estimate, the real assessment for Bengal would be 25,43,70,562 *dams*.[5] Assuming one rupee as equivalent to 40 *dams*, this would amount to about Rs 6.359 million. But James Grant, who had not noticed this error, put the figure for Bengal's assessed revenue at about Rs 10.69 million, a figure accepted without reservation by N.K. Sinha and Abdul Karim.[6] Prince Shah Suja, the second son of Emperor Shahjahan, conducted an assessment of Bengal's revenues in 1658. In it the assessed revenue was raised to about Rs 13.12 million.[7] Compared with the corrected figure of the assessed revenue in the *Ain*, this was a large rise, particularly in view of the well-merited contention that the price level was remarkably stable in Bengal (upon which we shall elaborate subsequently).

In order to understand the mode of revenue administration in Mughal Bengal, one should note an important point—that the role of *zamindars* in this province was not marginal or peripheral. The *zamindars*, who grew up under the Mughals were generally of two types: one, the kind who collected revenue according to the Mghal norms of assessment and collection, and paid revenue as *peshkash*, which was liable to be altered; two, the relatively independent *zamindars*, who collected revenue at rates fixed customarily or by themselves, and paid a fixed *peshkash* (tribute).[8] The second type conforms to Habib's description of *zamindars* of Bengal. It is worth quoting Habib in this regard: "Where the *zamindar* was called upon answer for the payment of land revenue within the area of his *zamindari*, he seems to have collected the land tax from the peasants at rates fixed by custom or by himself and to have paid the amount imposed on him, in turn by the administration. ...In the larger part of the Mughal empire on the other hand he was expected to collect the tax from the primary assesses (cultivators) in return simply for an allowance of one tenth, given either in cash or in allotment or revenue-free land."[9]

An important change took place in Bengal's revenue administration in the beginning of the 18th century. Murshid Quli Khan was appointed the *diwan* (governor) of the province in 1700. He transferred many of the Mughal *mansabdars* to Orissa and assigned the task of revenue collection for a major part of the province to *ijaradars* (revenue contractors). Out of these *ijaradars* emerged the *raj* families, which lasted fairly well till the introduction of the Permanent Settlement in 1793 by the English East India Company's government.[10] The six most important such families were the Burdan Raj, the Rajshahi Raj, the Dinajpur Raj, the Nadia Raj, the Birbhum Raj and the Bishnupur Raj. It may, however, be pointed out that not all of these *raj* families were creations of the 18th century. At least two families, namely Birbum Raj and the Bishnupur Raj, existed as independent tribute-paying principalities. The former ruled since the early Mughal days while the latter's history is traceable to even earlier times.[12] This suggests that the *mansabdari* system was definitely weaker in Bengal. In Todar Mal's revenue assessment, presented in the *Ain-i-Akbari*, the percentage of revenue from *khalisa* (meant for the Emperor's own treasury) lands was 59.33. According to James Grant's calculation, the corresponding figure in Murshid Quli's time was 76.71. It means that about Rs 10.9 million were meant for the imperial treasury. In the assessment that took place in between, the figure was 66.84.[13] Grant's figure comes very close to that of Salimullah, whe said that Rs 10.3 million rupees were annually sent from Mushidabad to the imperial treasury.[14] Considering the possible expenses of the *diwan's* household and the expenses on personal emplyees and forces, the two figures come remarkably close.

One point may be noted here. The percentage of *khalisa* lands in the Mughal empire as a whole was far lower than in Bangal. Tapan Rauchudhuri has suggested that 'the *khalisa*'s share in the total *jama* fluctuated between 5 per cent and 25 per cent.'[15] According to Irfan Habib, "In 1647, the estimated revenue of the *khalisa* amounted to about 13.6 per cent of the total."[16] But the share of *khalisa* lands in the assessment Bengal always exceeded 50 per cent, much higher than the average. From this, we can conclude that Bengal was always a much-coveted region as far as the imperial treasury was concerned.

We have noted the importance of *zamindars* in Bengal's rural economy, a point not disputed by any historian. What is of specific interest here is the role of these *zamindars* and *ijardars*—those who rose to prominence in the early 18th century—in the promotion of markets and the consequent expansion of the exchange economy. The *zamindars* were prominent in setting up local markets, *haats, bazaars* and *ganjs*. This act was necessary for the enforcement of local authority. Besides, these market places usually yielded good revenue.[17] These markets were supplemented by periodic fairs, which were centres of commerce, worship and pilgrimage. The *zamindars* were also voracious consumers of luxury goods imported by substantial merchants. Sometimes, specialized artisan villages grew up in response to the demand coming from the area where the seat of the Raja was located.[18]

Bengal's commercial pre-eminence in the 17th-18th centuries is well known. It might be argued that the growth of inter-regional commerce in the Mughal empire was partly due to the political and administrative integration of this province with the empire. This province was always a net exporter of rice, sugar and butter, supplying these articles to Agra, Coromandel and other regions in varying quantities. Tapan Raychaudhuri has pointed out, "Bengal rice was sent up the Ganges to Agra via Patna, to Coromandel and round the Cape to Kerala and various port towns on the west coast. ....In Bengal 'Butter', wrote Fryer, 'is in such plenty that although it be a bulky article to export, yet it is sent by sea to numberless places, it was also an item in the exports to Agra'. The export of sugar from Bengal by sea to 'all India' and by river to Agra and beyond was of great commercial importance."[19] Sanjay Subrahmanyam has also noted the role of Bengal rice in feeding the port town of Masulipatnam of north Coromandel as well as the cloth-producing villages of the Krishna delta in the second half of the 17th century. Bengal rice was exported in considerable amounts to the ports of Ceylon (now Sri Lanka) during the same period.[20] In the 18th century, the direct trade with Ceylon possibly went down, but ehre is evidence of export of large quantities of Bengal rice to Madras (now Chennai) and the neighbouring port of San Tome. The cheapness of Bengal's rice propelled the servants of the English Company to engage in this trade actively in the 18th century.[21] It may be pointed out that for rice, the ratio of cost of transport and price was higher than that for textiles. Hence, rice trade on such a scale suggests large price differentials as betwen Bengal and the importing regions, and extraordinary cheapness of rice in the former. The sugar of Bengal, as an 18th-century French trader noted, was sold in Surat and also exported to Persia and the Red Sea region.[22]

But it should be noted that Bengal's commercial superiority rested primarily not on foodstuffs like rice, sugar and butter, but on two other items, namely cotton textiles and raw silk. No discussion on Bengal's pre-colonial economy can proceed without saying something about these two premier trading items of Bangal.

The case of the cotton textile industry is an interesting pointer to the nature of Bengal's manufacturing base. While the towns and cities of upper India had their cotton-manufacturing establishments, there was little urban-centrism in Bengal's cotton-textile industry. While it should be conceded that there was some promotion of urbanization in Bengal under the Mughals, it is nevertheless true that its pace was much slower than in the Mughal core regions. But what is curious is that Bengal's cotton textile industry retained this character even when the Europeans had penetrated Bengal's extenal commerce significantly in the 18th century. The opinions of two distinguished scholars, namely N.K. Sinha and Sushil

Chaudhuri, are remarkably similar in this respect. What is remarkable is that the successive Maratha (*bargi*) raids could not alter this predominantly rural character of Bengal's cotton textile industry.[23] The traditional weaving caste in Bengal was named *tantubaya* or *tanti*, but with the expansion in production and marketing gradually other work-groups became engaged in spinning and weaving. While moving through Bengal in the 1720s, Robert Orme, the official historian of the English East India Company, found to his wonder that almost every inhabitant at any village lying beside a large town was engaged in the manufacture of cloth.[24] It should be kept in mind that these villages were not specialized weaving villages, but villages which combined agriculture with manufacturing activities. In the Coromandel region, the production of cloth for urban and external trade was done in strategically placed clusters of specialized weaving villages; in Bengal, there were numerous people who got engaged in cloth manufacture when agricultural activities were dull. As Professor Sushil Chaudhuri puts it succinctly, "labour from other activities could be drawn to weaving if and when necessary"[25].

A point should be noted about the nature of production. Location of the industry in the countryside was definitely one reason for the ability to produce cloth at low cost. The other reason was the low price of necessities in general and foodstuffs in particular. It might be argued that, notwithstanding regular exports of Bengal rice through coastal and river-borne trade, the price of rice was significantly lower in Bengal. Besides, the cost of transporting rice from peasants to artisans even when artisans were not cultivators themselves was practically zero or near zero, owing to the nature of location of the industry. When spinners and weavers have mixed occupations, combining cultivation with spinning or weaving, the imputed cost or shadow price of labour engaged in spinning and cloth manufacture would be low. That this was well observed by the officials of the English East India Company is characteristically revealed in a comment made by the Madras Council of the Company in a letter of 1661 written to the Court of Directors, "Neither may you ever expect the commodity can be made here to be afforded as reasonably as in Bengalah; for all provisions of victual, when at the cheapest, is here three times dearer than in Cassambazar and Hughly, where these taffetas are made, and consequently the weavers and other workmen employed therein can maintain themselves at two thirds less than shal be employed in this your town."[26] This statement, made in the early period of the English Company's involvement in India trade, speaks of the attention they had begun to pay to Bengal as a supplier of their main trading item, i.e. cotton texitles, to be procured from India and sold in Europe.

We may now turn to the question of source of raw materials of this industry. Fine cotton was produced in the district of Dacca. But there were considerable imports of raw cotton from distant areas such as the Surat–Burhanpur axis. The artisans of Burdwan and Birbhum (the latter a district relatively distant from the above-mentioned emporia) were important purchasers of Surat cotton. Bengal also used to import cotton yarn in substantial quantities from Surat during the period from the middle of the 17th and the early part of the 18th century.[27] Such transfer of raw cotton might be seen as one example of long-distance horizontal trade from one rural region to another.

Involvement of artisans in monetized exchanges can be understood from this fact of their compulsion to purchase raw materials, which could not be obtained by means of barter or through the *jajmani* system. When artisans need to purchase raw materials (raw cotton or yarn) to manufacture cloth, they have also to sell cloth not only to merchants engaged in long distance trade, but to other work-groups as well. When merchants make cash advances to artisans, the latter must have an irresistible tendency to make some profits out of such dealings. Such profits might not be sufficient to make them independent merchant-producers, but might lead them into greater involvement in the use of money. What is suggested here is that use of money need not have been confined to revenue payment.

On the rural production base of Bengal's manufactures, it can be noted that this phenomenon can be illustrated with reference to the production of raw silk as well. Production of raw silk involved two stages, cocoon-rearing and reeling. Both were rural activities conducted in peasant-cum-artisan households. In some cases, cocoons were immediately sold to merchants and in others, they were reeled into silk thread before being sold as wares. Tavernier, in the 1660s, noted the large-scale exports of raw silk to Ahmadabad and Surat and their conversion into fabrics there.[28] This silk trade with Gujarat continued well into the 18th century. Buying and selling activities on the part of the cocoon producers as well as reelers on a wide scale only imply that the degree of monetization was considerable and growing.

A few points that stand out in relation to the subject of monetization need to be mentioned. First of all, with the entry of the Europeans in Bengal's trade, the imperial mints of Dacca, Rajmahal and Karimabad did not prove equal to the task of providing enough silver coins, i.e. *sicca* rupees and *annas* for commerce. This paved the way for the circulation of other kinds of rupee currencies. The reasons for this alleged dearth of rupee currencies are, however, more complex than appear at first sight, and involve a number of other factors. It is true that a considerable amount of silver money went out of Bengal by way of tribute. In 1665, Tavernier met 110 ox-driven wagons, each containing 50,000 rupees, carrying Bengal's revenue to the imperial capital.[29] Such outflow might have caused a dearth of silver money for Bengal's commerce. One might feel tempted to liken it to the flight of Surat rupees to upper India. But one difference has also to be noted. A significant part of the supply of Surat goods came through upper India and this was one reason for the outflow of rupee currencies. But this was certainly not the case with Bengal, into which silver in the form of bullion and coins flowed regularly. It has been suggested that the huge amount of money regularly remitted to Delhi caused a scarcity of money.[30] But it is not clear how much of this remittance was in the form of physical movement of silver currency. With the rise of Jagat Seths in the early 18th century, the outflow of silver currency stopped and money was remitted through *hundis*. According to N.K. Sinha, this process started in the year 1728.[31] This was also the period when various rupee coins other than the imperial *sicca* began to circulate freely.

This abundance of money seems to the more stiking when cognizance is taken of the powerfully argued (by Om Prakash and Sushil Chaudhuri) case that there was remarkable price stability and there was no significant price trend.[32] Om Prakash's period of study starts with 1630 and ends with 1720. But Sushil Chaudhuri has argued that there was no significant price rise in the entire pre-colonial period, and has cautioned against possible misreading of Company records.[33] A more remarkable piece of information is provided by Syed Ezaz Hussain, who has argued that the price of rice, the staple food grain of the people, remained stable from the middle of the fourteenth century to the 1660s.[34] If Hussain's finding is considered correct, then the copying mistake in the *Ain*, pointed out by Habib, gives the impression that Bengal's revenue assessment rose very sharply during the period between Todar Mal and Shah Suja in real terms. This may be taken to mean that the importance of Bengal as a richly fertile and productive province had not been noticed prominently at the time of the Mughal conquest, and that this realization came later.

Very recently Shireen Moosvi, in line with the preconceptions of the Aligarh school, has suggested a large price increase of rice (from .58 rupees per *maund* to 1.48 rupees per *mound*—one *mound* is about 37.5 kg) during the period 1701-10 to 1741-50.[35] This is somewhat similar to Peter Marshall's opinion, "By the 1740s, however, Bengal's advantages (in respect of prices) seemed to be disappearing."[36] In Sushil Chaudhuri's view, Marshall's data source is very unreliable, and such sources should be treated more cautiously. Considering the nature of currencies in circulation in Bengal of that period, there are good reasons for the non-acceptance of the suggestions of Marshall and Moosvi. If the price of rice in terms of rupees had gone up so phenomenally, either of the two consequences would follow. One is a rise in the *cowrie* price of rupee. From the data on the exchange ratio between a rupee and *cowrie* collected by Frank Perlin, it seems that nothing like this happened.[37] Alternatively, the price of the *cowrie* in terms of goods would fall. This would reduce the profitability of the *cowrie* trade on the one hand, and render it increasingly unsuitable for exchange purposes on the other. But there is no evidence of any serious decline in imports of this shell. It is interesting that Peter Marshall, who has suggested a big price rise in the fourth decade of 18th-century Bengal, has also noted the existence a brisk *cowrie* trade about the same period.[38] So it is a legitimate surmise that whatever the validity or otherwise of the hypothesis of the 'price revolution' in the specific north Indian context, it is certainly not applicable in the case of Bengal.

Another interesting point concerns the condition of the money and credit market. Sushil Chaudhuri has shown that the rate of interest in Bengal was significantly higher than that in Surat and argued that it was due partly to the investment by Bengal merchants in bills drawn on Agra and partly to the failure of Europeans to obtain minting facilities.[39] This implies a relative shortfall in the supply of money, notwithstanding the largeness of the quantity of money in existence, in comparison with demand, at least in the short run. A higher rate of interest, on the other hand, generates a higher velocity of circulation of money and reduces the transaction's demand for money with a constant level of monetized output. In this case, the price level should rise in order to make good this reduction. But if this does not happen, the conclusion should be that the output of the monetized sector has expanded. On the other hand, the expansion of the monetized sector prevents a fall in the rate of interest with a fairly unchanged price level even if the stock of money in circulation grows. Here lies the primary theoretical justification for Shireen Moosvi's argument that the expansion of silk trade might have kept the rate of interest high in Bengal.[40] While the particular mention of silk trade, to the exclusion of other commercial activities, appears somewhat incomprehensible and hence questionable, it is quite possible that in the case of Bengal, the expansion of trading activities was the basic reason for the price stability along with a high rate of interest. Another reason for the high rate of interest may be conjectured. The structure of the money market often determines the rate of interest. The House of Jagat Seth governed the upper-level money market of Bengal, and it is not only possible but also probable that this lent a character to the market for money and credit that was less competitive than Surat or other low-interest regions. This might have been a factor in keeping the rate of interest at a high level.

Expansion of the monetized sector might be caused by two forces: one, reduction in the size of the non-monetized sector and two, an elastic supply-response to demand with a stable ratio between the monetized and non-monetized sector. It might well be that the expansion of the monetized sector in the relative sense as well as a growth of output prevented the price level from displaying an upward trend and kept Bengal's price advantage intact. Growth in demand from urban and external sources must have promoted some degree of specialization, and Professor Tapan Raychaudhuri has conceded the point by admitting the erosion of the *jajmani* system as far as the production for the medium and long-distance trade was concerned. Professor Raychaudhuri's comment, we have noted earlier, is made in the context of Mughal India as a whole. Here two points come out. First of all, what was true of Mughal India as a whole must not have been less true of Bengal, one of the most commercialized regions of the subcontinent. Two, that this full 'weaning away' did not occur abruptly, but took place as a long steadily moving process.

The question of elasticity of supply response needs a little reflaction. When the land-man ratio is favourable, and there is virtually little or no disguised unemployment, supply response may be elastic with some degree of population growth and consequent addition to the labour force in the case of agriculture even with a constant level of technology. In the case of the cotton textile industry, there was an additional advantage because of the rural and diffused character of production.

Now we can venture a few lines about the monetary system prevailing in pre-colonial Bengal. The mints at Dacca, Rajmahal and Murshidabad turned out *sicca* rupees and *muhrs*, but there was no Mughal copper mint. So, it was in essence a system of bimetallism, not trimetallism. Given that the general price level was lower in Bengal than in other states of India, it can be easily surmised that the quantity of *muhrs* turned out by the imperial mints was extermely small. The low-value transactions were dominated by the *cowrie* currency. In the 18th century, various kinds of rupees other than the Mughal *sicca* penetrated the economy of Bengal, and they became internalized in the exchange economy, particularly in the eastern part of Bengal. On the penetration of the *Arcot* rupee, the rupee minted by the English, the Dutch and the French in the name of the Nawab of Arcot, we can present the summary of a table about the cloth trade of Dacca in 1747. The figures are quoted in *Arcot* rupees. The total amount was Rs 28,50,000, out of which cloth worth Rs 4,00,000 went to the Emperor and the Nawab. The non-Europeans, taken together, accounted for 54 per cent of the total orders.[41] This shows that, besides the fact of the penetration of the *Arcot* rupee into the exchange economy of Bengal, Indian and other Asian traders had large shares of Bengal's external trade even in the late pre-colonial period.

We may now consider the peculiarities of urbanization in Bengal. In the 17th century, there were few towns in Bengal worth the name. Dacca, Rajmahal, Hooghly, Balasore and Kasimbazar were the important towns of Bengal. Among them, only Dacca was to some extent a manufacturing centre, besides being the capital city and a large centre of commerce. Hooghly and Balasore derived their importance from being port towns. Rajmahal had a mint and Kasimbazar was a mart of silk. Urbanization in the 18th century proceeded in two ways. One was the transfer of capital to Murshidabad and the growth of Calcutta (now Kolkata). Murshidabad developed into a large city in the first half of this century and by the 1750s had a population of 6 to 7 lakh. It developed into a large centre of silk trade and consumption. The large *zamindar* families of Bengal, many of whom grew into positions of power and wealth in the 18th century, furthered the process of urbanization by encouraging the settlement of armed forces, artisans and professional and artisans working under them. The towns of Burdwan, Krishnanagar, Natore, etc. were products of this period.[42]

We may now turn to some other features of the economy of pre-colonial Bengal. One was its importance to Europeans as a centre of trade. We have already noted that even in the late pre-colonial period, the importance of Indian and other Asian merchants in Bengal's external commerce was considerable. In the overseas trade, however, European companies and private traders had by then come to dominate. Tables 4.1 and 4.2 show the relative importance of Dutch and English East India Comapnies' imports from Bengal in the pre-colonial period.

TABLE 4.1 : Dutch E.E.C's imports from Bengal

Year	*Value (in 000 florins)*
1648–49	150.534
1658–59	1240.527
1668–69	1713.016
1678–79	1398.539
1688–89	1613.476
1698-99	3476.371
1708-09	2984.591
1718–19	4191.681

The linear trend equation is 1844.84 + 50.398 T with origin at 1683-84 and T unit = 10 years (owing to non-availability of data, the year 1717–18 has been taken for the following year).

[*Source*: Om Pradash: *The Dutch East India Company and the Economy of Bengal*, p. 70, Table 3.3]

TABLE 4.2 : The English E.E.C's Imports from Bengal

Year	Value (in 000 pound–sterling)
1670	25.358
1680	77.951
1690	3.970
1700	237.121
1710	173.819
1720	332.792
1730	431.581
1740	401.163
1750	511.177

The linear trend equation is y= 143.87 + 58.85 T with origin at 1710 and T unit = 10 years

[*Source*: K.N. Chaudhuri, *The Trading World of Asia and the English East India Company*, Table C.2]

As per Om Prakash's calculations, the proportion of precious metals to the total value of imports into Bengal by the Dutch E.E.C. varied from a minimum of 47 per cent in 1687 to a maximum of 97 per cent 1717. In the fifty years during the period 1663–1717, for which the figures are given (the figures for a few years are not given) by Om Prakash, the proportion for thirty separate years lies within the range of 60 to 90 per cent. Among the other twenty, the figures for fifteen are found to be above 90 per cent. Only five of the total number of years show a proportion below 60 per cent.[43]

K.N. Chaudhuri has not given figures for imports of precious metals into Bengal. But from the figures given by him on the imports of the English Company's treasures into Asia, it is seen that during 1660–1760, the proportion of treasures was between 60 to 90 per cent in 88 years separately. For three successive years—1703, 1704 and 1705—treasures constituted the whole. For 1759 and 1760, the proportion reached the abnormally low figures of 32.4 per cent and 27.8 per cent respectively.[44] The reasons for this will be discussed in Chapter 6.

These figures highlight two features. One is that, although as we have indicated, Asian merchants had a considerable share of pre-colonial Bengal's trade in the 18th century, there were large demands for Bengal's goods on the part of European Companies. Second, their imports into Bengal consisted overwhelmingly of treasure. It seems that for her necessary imports like raw cotton, Bengal had to rely principally on Asian merchants. One may find it alluring to attempt a comparison of the economic situation of pre-colonial Bengal with that of contemporary Gujarat. Such an attempt has a justification in the sense that Bengal and Gujarat were the two leading commercial regions of the Mughal empire, and contributed in large measure to the prosperity of Mughal India. In both the regions, on the other hand, there were significant departures in the pattern of use of money from the imperial system of trimetallism. Both regions had their own non-metallic currency media. Bengal had her *cowrie*, while Gujarat had *badam*. In Gujarat, there was widespread circulation of *mahmudi*, while in

Bengal, the silver coin named *Narainy*, minted in the tributary kingdom of Coochbihar, was current in some parts of the province.

Surat's overseas trade till the early 18th century was dominated by Indian merchants, and there were merchant princes like Vriji Vora, and then Haji Ahmad Chellaby and Abdul Gafur.[45] In Bengal, such merchant princes were absent, but there were big merchants like Omichand and Kwaja Wahid.[46] On the other hand, Bengal witnessed the rise of the largest banking family of subcontinent, namely the House of Jagat Seths.

Some other differences in respect of trade and traders are noticeable. As we have noted earlier, Mughal noblemen often took an active interest in water-borne trade. This was much more prominent in the case of Bengal than Surat. In fact, after the withdrawal of the Mughals from the shipping business of Bengal in the early 18th century, overseas trade by merchants stationed in Bengal became confined only to journeys to and from the Maldives.[47] Involvement by state officials in overseas trade on such a scale is not to be found in Surat's long history of maritime trade, although Surat was the major port of the Indian subcontinent from about 1550 and she retained her importance for nearly two centuries.

The respective behaviour of the money markets of the two regions towards European commerce also suggests some interesting points of differnece. We can here take as a reference the situation that developed in Gujarat in the wake of the breakdown of the Mughal empire. Following Ashin Dasgupta's meticulous account, four reasons for the decline of Surat as the most important port of India can be delineated: (i) fleecing activities of the Mughal nobility and plunder by the Marathas, (ii) fall of the Safavid dynasty in Persia in 1722, which meant he loss of the big Persian market, (iii) civil war in Yemen and the pressure brought on Indian merchants by the warring groups, (iv) blockade of the city by the warships of the English East India Company.[48] Besides, the disruption of trade routes caused a rupture between Surat and its hinterland in north India. According to recent research, the operation of the money merchants, belonging mostly to the *Bania* community, was geared to the commercial needs of the English East India Company in the wake of the decline of Surat. While the English Company faced there a serious crisis of credit, the only viable alternative the *Banias* could hope for was the protection given by the Company authorities of Bombay and Surat. The result was a rather smooth transition, sometimes interspersed by conflicts over rates of exchange, to an Anglo-*Bania* order of imperial expansion.[49]

The process of transition in Bengal was not as smooth as that in Gujarat. Bengal's shipping came to be dominated by Europeans after the cessation of Mughal involvement and often goods of Indian merchants were carried in ships owned by Europeans.[50] However, this European dominance hardly affected the money market. As we have already pointed out, borrowing from Bengal's money market was a problem that continuously plagued the English East India Company throughout the 17th and the first half of the 18th century. Gradually an atmosphere of collaboration develped, but it was ridden with conflicts, as we shall have occasions to discuss. It might be that the money merchants' drive for profits and the scope of expansion of their business offered by the English Company's demand for credit was instrumental in giving birth to the atmosphere of collaboration, but it was hardly similar to the Anglo-*Bania* order that came into being in western India. Only when the English East India Company, eight years after the Battle of Plassey, assumed the *diwani* (revenue administration) of Bengal could it acquire the loyalty of a new class of money merchants, but the merchants having firmer roots in the economy could not be easily subjugated, because they did not have much need of protection from the Company.

Now let us come to the nature of the currency order in pre-colonial Bengal. We have already remarked on the dearth of *sicca* rupees and the penetration of other kinds of rupee coins. This was a big problem faced by the early colonial administrators of Bengal. The *Arcot* rupees we have already referred to had different varieties, and *sicca* rupees, owing to differences in the years of production and variations in the names of mints, did not command the same market value. It was reported from Dacca in 1787 that there were 52 such different varieties of *sicca* rupees in circulation in the district, although the predominant currency was the *Arcot* rupee of different varieties.[51] One can easily understand that this multiplicity of currencies in circulation was a legacy of the pre-colonial era. The example of Dacca was not an isolated one. To a greater or lesser extent, this situation prevailed throughout Bengal.

In pre-colonial Bengal, there was no copper mint even in 1700.[52] This year incidentally belonged to a period when the Dutch East India Company was importing large amounts of copper into Bengal. For example, the Dutch brought Rs 13983 worth of Japanese copper into Bengal in the year 1701-02. For later years, these figures were much higher. In 1710-11, Rs 29,748 worth of copper was imported.[53] We cannot say how this copper was used, but it is certain that it did not go to the mints of Bengal.

Why the copper coin of the Mughals could not make any inroads into the exchange economy of Bengal, while the *sicca* rupee and its fractional piece *anna* did so substantially, is a mystery, but it was nevertheless a fact. The low-priced transactions, i.e., all the ransactions below the level of the *anna*, were conducted in *cowrie*. This was not a feature unique to the 17th-18th centuries. The tradition of use of *cowrie* in Bengal was very old, and a noted Bengali historian has described it in the following language: "Even in the Gupta period, when gold, silver and copper coins were in wide circulation, the lowest standard currency was *cowrie*, Fa-hien wrote in the 4th century that people used *cowrie* only in sales and purchases. In the *Charyapada* (of the 10th-11th centuries), we find use of *kabadi (cowrie)* and *bodi (buri)*. On the expedition of Turks, Minhaj-ud-din has said that the advancing Turks nowhere saw rupee coins in circulation in Bengal, and *cowrie* was used in day-to-day transactions. Even royal donations were made in *cowries*, the lowest donation of King Laxman Sen being 100,000 *cowries*. Elsewhere too, we find evidence of circulation of *cowrie* in the 13th century. Ma Huan, in the fifteenth century, produces the same evidence. The evidence of the medieval Bengali literature and foreign travelers is also alike. In 1750 too, English merchants saw revenue collection in *cowrie* in the city of Calcutta: *cowrie* was also the medium of exchange in ordinary acts of purchase and sale in markets."[54] (italics added) It may be mentioned that the *Charyapada* is the earliest known specimen of Bengali literature. Combined with the fact of a pluralistic order in the sphere of circulation of rupees, this observation serves to highlight a point; a pluralism in the money market at the upper level coexisted in the 18th century with a uniformity at the lower level. So, it can be argued that the erosion of this type of pluralism, along with the conflict in this area, and the decline of the *cowrie* form two important and interesting aspects of monetary transition in the province of Bengal in the colonial period. These two aspects we propose to discuss in the next two chapters.

NOTES AND REFERENCES

1. Sarkar, Jadunath. *History of Bengal.* Reprint. Patna : 1973 (First Published from Dacca, 1949) : 180–187.
2. Deyell. "Akbar's Currency System and Monetary Integration of the Conquered Kingdoms. In *The Imperial Monetary System of Mughal India.* Ed. J.F. Richard. O.U.P., 1987 : 30.
3. Grant, James. Analysis of the Finances of Bengal, Appendix 4 to *The Fifth Report from the Select Committee of the House of Commons on the Affairs of the East India Company.* Ed : W.T. Firminger. New York (reprint), 1969.
4. W.H. Moreland, after an examination of Grant's analysis, made a very pertinent remark, "it is not inconceivable that Akbar's administrators should have adopted, from the outset, methods entirely at variance with their usual practice, and established in Bengal a revenue demand not alterable from year to year; but it seems to me much more probable that those peculiar features of Bengal developed gradually under the pressure of exceptional circumstances, until figures which were originally prepared for use in granting assignments became eventually a standard of the recurring demand on the Intermediaries, not liable to alteration, but liable to be supplemented by the cesses in the way Grant describes. On this view, we should regard the revisions made by Shah Suja and Jafar Khan as corrections of

this original valuation, incorporating the territory which had been acquired in the interval, and whose increments of the figures for particular areas which had been made from time to time." Moreland: *Agrarian System of Moslem India.* Delhi : Oriental Books Reprint Corporation, 1968 (First Published in 1929).

5. Habib, Irfan, *An Atlas of the Mughal Empire.* Delhi : O.U.P., 1986: Table 1.
6. Sinha, N.K. *Economic History of Bengal,* Vol. 2. Kolkata: Firma K.L. Mukhopadhyay, 1962 : 1.
   Karim, Abdul. "Mughal Revenue System". In *History of Bangladesh,* Vol. 2. Ed. Sirajul Islam. Dacca: Asiatic Society of Bangladesh, 1992 : 166.
7. Karim : Ibid, 165–167.
8. A lucid account of this distinction is to be found in Aniruddha Ray, *Mughal Amaler Zamidar O Banglar Taludar* (The *Zamindar* of the Mughal Period and the Talukdar of Bengal) in Ray (ed.) *Madhyajuger Bharat* : Kolkata : K.P. Bagchi, 1987 : 25–44.
9. Habib, Irfan. Agrarian Relations and Land Revenue. *C.E.H.I., I.* Ch. IX(1) : 245.
10. Sarkar, Jadunath, op. cit., 408–440 passim.
11. These six families, taken together, accounted for about half of the total land revenue of Bengal at the time of the Permanent Settlement introduced by the English Company in 1793. vide, Sirajul Islam: *The Permanent Settlement in Bengal, 1790–1819.* Dacca : Bangla Academy, 1979 : 3, Table 1.
12. For a history of the Birbhum Raj, Ranjan Gupta: *Rahrer Samaj, Arthaniti O Gana Bidroha* (The Society, Economy and Popular Rebellion in the Rahr Region). Kolkata : Subarnarekha, 2001 : 32–35.
    For a brief account of the Bishnupur Raj, Islam, Ibid. 135–40.
13. Grant, James. Analysis of the finances of Bengal, 189–91.
14. Karim, Abdul. Mughal Revenue System.... 167.
15. Raychaudhuri, Japan. The State and Economy. *C.E.H.I.* I, Ch. VII(1) : 178.
16. Habib, Irfan. Potentialities.... *Essays in Indian History,* 188.
17. For a good account, Sen, Sudipta. *The Empire of Free Trade.* Ch. 1: 19–59 passim.
18. We can, for example, name a weaving village Tantipara, which specialized in the production of silk cloth and had flourished during the days of the Birbhum Raj and catered largely to the demand from the establishment of the Raja. Gupta, Ranjan. *Rahrer Samaj Arthaniti O Gana Bidroha.* 363–63.

19. Raychaudhuri, Tapan Inland Trade, *C.E.H.I.* I, Ch. XI : 330–31.
20. Subrahmanyam. "Rural Industry and Commercial Agriculture in Late Seventeenth Century South-Eastern India". *Past and Present.* (February 1990): 90–108.
    Arasaratnam, S. "Rice Trade in Eastern India, 1650–1740". *M.A.S.* 22, no. 3 (1988) : 537–38.
21. Arasaratnam. Ibid, 541–545.
22. Ray, Indrani. India in Asian Trade in the 1730s: A Discussion by a French Trader, Barun De (ed): *Essays Presented to Prof S.C. Sarkar*, Delhi : People's Publishing House, 1776 : 223–24.
23. Sinha. *Economic History of Bengal.* Vol. 1. Kolkata : 1961. 'In the eighteenth century the weavers of cotton-piece goods occupied the most important position in Bengal's economy. During the period under review we do not come across those *karkhanas* or big workshops of which we hear so much in the days of the Great Mughals. Nor do we find weavers concentrated in European settlements, though the Europeans were the chief buyers of the cloth woven by them. The Court of Directors, as also its servants in Bengal, tried to encourage weavers to reside under their protection within the bounds of Calcutta. The Directors hoped that this would give their servants an opportunity of having many if not most of the goods under their immediate inspection. But the response was vary inadequate. Even before this, at the time of the Bargi incursions into Western parts of Bengal, when most of the wealthy people in the affected parts of Bengal thronged to the security of the British settlements in Calcutts, the weavers from Western Bengal fled mainly to established centres of industry in north Bengal. But in spite of this localization, cotton weaving was, in the main, a rural domestic industry throughout this period.' (italics added) Ibid, 157.
24. Sarkar, Smritikumar. "Social Organization of Artisan Production in India: Changing Role of the Market, Technology and Merchant Creditor". In *Economic History of India from Eighteenth to Twentieth Century.* Ed. Binay Chaudhuri. Delhi : Centre for Studies in Civilizations, 2005, p. 168.
25. Chaudhuri, Sushil. *From Prosperity to Decline—Bengal in the Eighteenth Century.* Delhi : Manohar, 1995 : 135.
26. Cited in Chaudhuri, K.N. *The Trading World of Asia Cambrige and the English East India Company.* C.U.P., 1978 : 248–89.
27. *From Prosperity to Decline....*, p. 256, Raychaudhuri, Tapan. Non-agricultural Production. *C.E.H.I.* I, Ch. X(1) : 271.

28. Tavernier. *Travels in India,* Book 2V. Ed. Ball. Delhi : Munshiram Manoharlal, 1995 : 2.
29. Idem : Travels in India, Book 1, 92–93.
30. Jadunath., Sarkar. *History of Bengal....* 373–74.
31. Sinha, N.K. *Itihas Gabeshana* (Selected Bengali Writings of N.K. Sinha), Kolkata: K.P. Bagchi. 1988 : 69.
32. Prakash, Om. *The Dutch East India Company....,* 248–255.
    Sushil Chaudhuri : *Trade and Commercial Organization in Bengal* 1640–1720, Firma K.L. Mukhopadhyay, Kolkata: 1976 : 241–48.
    In his *From Prosperity to Decline,* Chaudhuri suggests a reinterpretation of the absence of inflation, differing from his earlier monetarist explanation and concurring broadly with the opinion of Om Prakash. vide Chaudhuri, Ibid, 278–305.
33. Chaudhuri, Sushil. "General Economic Conditions under the Nawabs". *History of Bangladesh,* Vol. 1. Ed. Sirajul Islam....51–53.
34. Hossain, Syed Ezaz. *The Bengal Sultanate—Politics, Economy and Coins.* Delhi : Manohar, 2003 : 291–92.
35. Moosvi, Shireen. "The Indian Economic Experience 1600–1900; A Quantitative Study". *The Making of History, Essays Presented to Irfan Habib.* Delhi: Tulika, 2000 : 342, Table 13.
36. Marshall, Peter. *East India Fortunes; The British in Bengal in the Eighteenth Century.* Oxford: O.U.P., 1976 : 35.
37. Perlin. Money Use in Late Pre-colonial India... Appendix 5.1.
38. Marshall. *East Indian Fortunes....* 86.
39. Chaudhuri, Sushil. "The Financing of Investments in Bengal 1650–1720". *I.E.S.H.R.* 8, no. 2 (1971): passim.
    Idem. "European Companies and the Export Trade in the Eighteenth Century". In *History of Bangladesh,* Volume 1. Ed. Sirajul Islam. passim.
40. Moosvi, Shireen. A Note on Interest rates in the Seventeenth and Early Eighteenth Centuries. In *Money and Credit in Indian History.* Ed. Amiya Kumar Bagchi. Delhi : Tulika, 2002 : 90.
41. Iftikar-ul Awwal. "The State of Indigenous Industries". In *History of Bangladesh,* Volume 1. Ed. Sirajul Islam. .... 290.
42. Ahmed, Sharifuddin. "Urbanization and Urban Classes". Ibid, Vol. 2, 206–07.
43. Calculated from Om Prakash : *The Dutch E.E.C.* ...Table 3.2, 66–67.
44. Calculated from K.N. Chaudhuri: *The Trading World of Asia....* Table C.4 : 512.
45. For an account of Vriji Vora, vide W.H. Moreland: *From Akbar*

to Aurangzeb, Reprint. Delhi : Munshiram Manoharlal, 1990 : 152–58.

For Chellaby and Gafur, vide Dasgupta, Ashin. "The Merchants of Surat". In *Elites of South Asia.* Eds. Edmund Leach and S.N. Mukherjee. C.U.P., 1970: passim.

46. For Khwaja Wazid and Omichand, vide Footnote 103 to Ch. 2
47. Prakash, Om. The Indian Maritime Merchant.... 451.
48. Dasgupta, Ashin. *Indian Merchants and the Decline of Surat* 1700–1750. Weisbaden, 1976 : particularly the Introduction, 1–35 passim.
49. Subrahmanian, Laksmi. "Banias and the British; the Role of Indigenous Credit in the Process of Imperial Expansion in Western India in the Second Half of the Eighteenth Century". *M.A.S.* 21, no. 3 (1987) : 473–510, passim.
    Subrahmanian's excellent and detailed account does not suggest any general intransigence on the part of the Banias.
50. Marshall, Peter. *East Indian Fortunes....* 85–116.
51. Mitra, Debendra Bijay. *Monetary System in the Bengal Presidency* 1757–1835. Kolkata: 1991 : 76–78.
52. Habib, Irfan. *An Atlas of the Mughal Empire....* Sheet 11B, 49.
53. Calculated from Prakash, Om. *The Dutch E.E.C.* ....Table 5.2, 134.
54. Ray, Nihar Ranjan. *Bangalir Itihas, Adi Parba* (A History of the Bengali People, Early Phase). Reprint. Kolkata: Pashchimbanga Niraksharata Durikaran Samity, 1980 : 206.

Chapter Five

Sarrafs and Bankers in the Transitional Economy of Bengal

This chapter studies briefly the changing conditions of the *sarrafs* and bankers of Bengal during the transition period. *Sarrafs* or *shroffs* were essentially moneychangers, whose main business was to test the purity of coins and to exchange one coin for another. They also exchanged bullion for currencies, and vice versa. In a wider sense, the category *sarraf* included moneylenders and bankers, who accepted deposits and transferred funds from one place to another by means of *hundis*, i.e. bills of exchange and promissory notes. A distinguished student of Indian monetary and commercial history has elegantly and succinctly outlined the mode of operation of the *hundi* business in these words: "Broadly speaking, two modes existed. The first was to draw money from a *sarraf* against a promise to pay him in another town when the *hundi* was produced there. The alternative was to pay money down, with a promise from the *sarraf* that the money would be recovered in the other town, once the *hundi* was produced. In the former case, the *sarraf's* charges were higher than in the latter, since first, the risk now devolved more on him, and second because there was a time element, (and hence an implicit loan involved)."[1] It should be added that the mode of operation of *hundis* had direct bearing on the money market. As a recent writer has put it, "When the *hundi* carried a statement promising payment within a stipulated time... the conversion of credit into cash was regulated by the details mentioned herein. But if the *hundi* was made payable to the bearer, the conversion of credit into cash was freed from the constraint of time and place. the *hundi* thus became saleable at a small discount, which accounted for the gain of the buyer whose cash was locked."[2] It goes without saying that such *hundis* added to the supply of money. It should be added that the growing *hundi* business increased the velocity of circulation of money in pre-colonial India. It may not be out of place to suggest that the evidence on the growth of *hundi* business and its probable impact on the money market somewhat weaken the force of the Aligarh formulation of the 'price revolution', in the sense that it destroys empirically the simplistic assumption of a straight relation between the supply of metallic currency and the price level, because *hundis* circulated as near money, although they were not perfect susbstitutes for modern bank notes.

On the growth of this business, the evidence is perhaps overwhelming. Tavernier noted in the 1660s, "In India, a village must be very small indeed if it has not a moneychanger called a *shroff*, who acts as banker to make remittances of money and issue letters of exchange. As, in general, these changers have an understanding with the Governors of Provinces, they enhance the rupee as they please for *paisa* and *paisa* for these shells."[3] What is suggested here in fact in the existence of several layers of *sarrafs*, because a village-level *sarraf* is not in general supposed to have a close liaison with a provincial governor. In the available studies on the commercial economy of pre-colonial India, one can find numerous references to the operation of these moneychangers and bankers. One can refer to the *hundis* drawn at Agra on Surat in the 17th century, particularly during 1620-1660, when large quantities of goods used to reach Surat via upper India. Surat merchants needed to transfer funds to Agra for making their purchases and so, those bills carried a premium. On the other hand, bills drawn at Surat on Agra carried a discount. The reason was that Agra was a major centre of procurement of goods that were to come to Surat and be used for overseas trade.[4] It may be mentioned that *hundi* networks were extensively used by Mughal officials also. Irfan Habib, in his celebrated paper on the potentialities of capitalist development in Mughal India, has aptly observed that orders of payment of salaries to troops could also be commercial paper, discounted by *sarrafs*.[5] We can also refer to the well-studied case of Bangal merchants' profitable investment in Agra bills, which reportedly caused a scarcity of currency in Bengal's money market, much to the inconvenience of the European trading companies.[6] Such examples can be multiplied. As Tapan Raychaudhuri has suggested, "As a market for these fully saleable *hundis* developed, they provided a channel for investment."[7]

The rates of discount or premium ostensibly depended on the respective liquidity positions of the two places, one where the *hundi* is drawn and the other where it is received. Irfan Habib refers to an episode of the late 17th century, in which the exchange rate of bills drawn at Patna on Agra rose from Rs $98\frac{1}{8}$ to Rs $98\frac{3}{8}$ per 100 rupees, in consequence of the delivery of Rs three lakh to Patna *sarrafs* by the outgoing Mughal governor for payment in Agra.[8] How *hundis* could sometimes serve as book money is illustrated in an interesting passage, "Suppose a person having paid a fixed sum at the port of Surat to a *saffar* (banker) of that place, brings a hundi, which in Persian is called *sufta*, drawn by him (the *sarraf*) on his partner or agent at Ahmadabad, he may, if he chooses, collect cash, paying the deduction on account of *anth* (conversion of bill money into coin) or in case another person has a claim against the possessor of the bill (*hundawi*) for that sum, he may give it to that person, and free himself from that obligation. Similarly he (the new holder of the bill) may transfer it to another, untill it reaches a person against whom the drawee of the *hundawi* has claims, and who, therefore, surrendering it to the latter, relieves himself of his debt. But cash is not used throughout."[9] Of course *sarrafs* had other functions and had other instruments of control over the money market. Urban *sarrafs* often had close liaison with imperial mints. One relatively less known example can be cited to illustrate the point. One of the major Mughal mints, namely that of Surat, was farmed out to a few *sarrafs* who operated the mint, each with a team[10] This was, however, a deviation from the standard Mughal practice. Yet the connection between *sarrafs* and mints is undeniable. The hold of the legendary

House of the Jagat Seth over the mint of Murshidabad is well known, which we shall discuss later. The *sarrafs* used to keep inventories of coined money and merchants, native as well as foreign, had to rely on them when the time constraint in the coining of bullion became too binding. As one authority puts it in the context of the Dutch Company's dependence of the *sarrafs* of Bengal in this regard: "A mint would take weeks, or even months, to deliver even relatively moderate sums of money, obliging the Company to borrow in the money market in the meantime and incur an interest cost. The *sarrafs* ordinarly made an on-the-spot payment, though on occasions they asked for time up to two months or an arrangement involving payment in two instalments. In such cases, if the Company was not in a position to wait, it had no option but to accept a somewhat lower price from another *sarraf* willing to make an immediate full payment."[11] (italics original)

Such examples show that the *sarrafs* became a conspicuous class of surplus appropriators in the mercantile world of pre-colonial India. It might be surmised that the *sarrafs* had a relation with domestic merchants, similar to those with Europeans. The entry of Europeans into direct Indian trade only diversified their operations and strengthened their bargaining power. It is quite natural that the specialized *sarrafs* had a relation of mutual complementarity and conflict with the goods' merchants, because a higher rate of discount would harm the business of the latter. Irfan Habib refers to an incident in Ahmadabad in the early 18th century, when the *sarrafs* raised the rate of deduction on account of *anth,* and merchants nearly took to arms, finally securing a reduction in the rate of discount.[12]

There were other sources of *sarrafs'* profits. In a monetary system, where there were no legally fixed ratios among different coins, it was possible for *sarrafs* to create artificial scarcities of this or that particular coin and push up its prices. In regions where there was a multiplicity in the circulation of currencies, the scope of the *sarrafs'* operation was conceivably larger. Bengal in the 18th century was precisely such a region. In Bengal's trading centres, rupees of different mints, even if of the same quality and standard, had different demands. So the rupee that was foremost in demand commanded a premium over others in spite of being of the same weight and finesse, and in the process of exchange there was a profit accruing to *sarrafs*. Besides, *sarrafs* could make profits by recoinage of old coins. One prominent example was the recoinage of *sonaut* rupees into *siccas*. In Mughal India, all the rupees coined under the regional ruler, king or nawab, were called *siccas*. After three years of circulation, a *sicca* rupee was called *sonaut* and passed at 111/116th of th originally denominated value. *Sarrafs* accepted these *sonauts* for recoinage and took out money from their owners. This practice prevailed because revenue was received in new rupees, which most of the revenue payers did not usually have in their possession, making it necessary for them to turn to *sarrafs,* who had a close liaison with the mint masters.

The *sicca* rupee was the dominant coin in the western part of Bengal. In eastern Bengal, various kinds of other rupees were current in the periods of the nawabs. The most prominent of them were *Arcot* rupees (rupees coined in the name of the Nawab of Arcot) of various kinds. European companies also coined *Arcot* rupees and so there were English *Arcots,* Dutch Arcots, French *Arcots,* etc. Besides, the *Narainy* currency, worth less than half a *sicca* rupee, was very much in circulation. It goes without saying that such pluralism in the coin market provided an ideal situation for the money-changing *sarrafs* to thrive. One feature of the currency situation in pre-colonial India was the difference in the regional acceptability of particular coin types. The value of a particular currency was a function of the distance between its place of production and place of circulation. The phenomenon may be illustrated with reference to a letter written in 1712 by the Bengal servants of the English East India Company, stating that the *sicca* rupees produced at the Mughal mints of Surat, Dacca, Patna and Cuttuck fetched less value than the Murshidabad rupees at Hooghly, although those rupees were of the same weight and fitnesse.[13] It goes without saying that to *sarrafs* holding stocks of Murshidabad rupees, it was an added advantage.

No discussion on Bengal *sarrafs* and bankers of the pre-colonial period is meaningful without a reference to the great banking house of the Jagat Seths. Prof N.K. Sinha estimated their assets to be of the order of Rs fourteen crore (140 million) in the 1750s.[14] Considering the price level and the supposed nominal value of the gross national product of that period, this must be a gigantic sum indeed. Whether the Seths had a monopoly of the minting rights in Murshidabad might be debatable,[15] but it is well known that they made extensive use of the mint. The credit-hungry European companies, which were often in need of short-term loans for their puchanses, called 'investments' (it was not investment in real capital, but in money) in those days, were very much dependent on this house for money. This house, on the other hand, found in the demand coming from these companies a profitable channel of investment of their wealth. Besides controlling the mints, the house received revenues from *zamindars* on behalf of the Nawab of Bengal's treasury and often stood security for them. They also controlled the rates of *buttu* (discount) on different kinds of currencies circulating in Bengal. Their control over the urban money market of Bengal was so profound that no money merchant or bullion dealer dared offer a higher price than the Seths to European companies for silver bullion.

The picture of the *sarrafs* and bankers in pre-colonial Bengal cannot be complete without taking into account the less wealthy *sarrafs* and bankers, who were not as powerful as the Jagat Seths but who operated in various large, medium and small centres of commerce. In the early colonial period, these *sarrafs* became important in the money market because of their determined opposition to the policy measures of the colonizing rulers. The Jagat Seths, however enormous their wealth might have been, were after all the product of a situation in which money-changing and banking activities flourished vigorously. The situation naturally produced numerous *sarrafs* and bankers of lesser fame. In order to understand the monetary transition in Bengal, we have to understand the roles of these *sarrafs* and bankers. They advanced credit to businessmen, tested the quality of coins and exchanged them at a discount and purchased bullion and coins. Their role in pre-colonial Bengal's monetary economy was by no means insignificant. It can be surmised that *sarrafs* dealing in rupee coins only operated generally at urban centres of commerce, in which various types of rupee coins came for circulation and were exchanged with one another.

But in Bengal, low-value exchanges were dominated by the *cowire* currency, and there was hardly any copper coin in circulation in the 17th-18th centuries. Here we have to recocile the story of the prosperity of Bengal's *sarrafs* with the circulation of this currency. It is clear that wealthy Bengal *sarrafs* qua *sarrafs* dealt in rupees and sometimes in gold coins and operated in urban and entrepot centres of commerce. But one section of *sarrafs* must have operated in the rural markets, i.e. *haats* (periodic markets held once or twice a week) and *bazars* (more regular markets). They were called *potdars.* About a century before Tavernier's sighting of the exchange between *paisas* and *cowries* in Agra, *Chandimangal,* a Bengali poetic work written in the second half of the 16th century, had referred to a class of *potdars* exchanging gold, silver coin (but not any copper coin) and *cowrie.* The mode of operation of these *potdars* has been described in the course of story telling. In one of these tales, Kalketu, a poor village hunter (*byadh*), got a gold ring from the goddess Chandika, who had gone to his house incognito and made this gift. When the hunter went to the *potdar* to sell it, the latter offered a price of six hundred and sixty (eight *pans* and five *gandas*) *cowries.* But then the cunning *potdar* heard a commanding voice from the heaven, and afraid that the curse of the goddess would fall on him, gave the hunter seven crores of *takas,* the basic silver coins (probably the pre-Mughal silver coins)[16]. This mythical episode lays bare a fact of the monetary economy of the then Bengal, the fact of the existence of a class of money-changers who traded in gold, silver and *cowrie.*

As we shall see later, imports of *cowrie* was a profitable business to Indian as well as European mechants, although not all types of merchants participated in this trade in equal measure. It is not unreasonable to argue, in the light of this profitable business, which continued well enough in the 18th century,[17] that exchange of rupees with *cowrie* and vice versa was a source of profit to the *sarrafs.* It can be inferred that the more substantial *cowrie*-dealing *sarrafs* got their stocks from domestic mechants who used to sell goods to *cowrie*-importing traders. Agents of big merchants and European companies needed *cowries,* along with rupees, for procurement of goods, and they conceivably received these shells from these *sarrafs*. There was another class of cowrie-dealing *sarrafs,* who operated at the lowest rung of the ladder of money-changing business and dealt with small rural hucksters. In the year 1770, about two centuries after the period of Chandimangal, it was seen that in village *haats* a class of *potdars* was sitting with stocks of *cowrie.* In the early part of the day, the hucksters took cowrie from them in exchange of rupees, and in the afternoon, they would bring back their *cowrie* and go away with the rupees. During that period, a well-organized *haat* named *Chandpara* of the district of Murshidabad had three *cowrie* shops.[18] A report of 1775 about a *tarf* Rangamati of the district of Murshdabad had three *cowrie* shops in a *haat;* besides there were two other *sarrafs.*[19] In this connection, it can be said that, as discussed earlier, the price of rice, the chief agricultural product of Bengal, was extremely low, and traders—Indian and Europeans—continued to take rice to south India and Ceylon, without caring much for the cost of transport. Rice, along with coarse cloth, was probably the principal item of trade in the rural *haats* of Bengal, and the low price of rice leads to the surmise that rural transactions were largely dependent on the circulation of this medium and that this phenomenon gave the *cowrie*-holding *sarrafs* and *cowrie* shops, permanent as well as temporary, a significant place in the rural monetary economy of pre-colonial Bengal.

Evidence of such shops from urban areas is, however, not found, at least for the 18th century. Of course, this is not to suggest that the *cowrie* currency circulated exclusively in the rural areas. There are reports of the Fort William Council paying daily wages to coolies in *cowries* in the 1750s.[20]

To sum up, we may delineate three categories of *sarrafs* functioning in the money markets of pre-colonial Bengal. At the bottom were the petty, subsistence-earning village *sarrafs* whose clients were hucksters (pedlars), peasants and village artisans. There was a middle category of *sarrafs* operating usually in urban and intermediate *ganj*-level markets and dealing with urban merchants or their agents who required locally circulating rupee currencies and cowries for the procurement of merchandise. At the apex lay the larger wealth accumulating *sarrafs* who, besides money-changing, were engaged in discounting bills of exchange for large-scale transfer of funds. These *sarrafs* combined money-changing with deposit banking.

We may here digress a little and note some more points about the House of Jagat Seths, because they might help us in understanding the relation between native *sarrafs* and bankers and the European Companies. Before the Battle of Plassey, the relation of the House of Jagat Seths with the European Companies was one of collaboration, but the former dictated the terms. The Seths needed the Europeans but the latter, particularly the Englhish, needed the Seths more. Occasionally, the Seths interceded on behalf of the English. For example, when some conflicts of the English Companies men with Nawab Shuja-ud-din's guards at checkpoints threatened to stop the Company's business, the Jagat Seth interceded and pacified and Nawab by offering a handsome sum of money.[21] But the house often coerced the English into paying back in due time the money they had lent to the Company and this coercion usually took the form of a threat of suspension of business.[22] The English obtained the *farman* of 1717 from Emperor Farukhshiyar, granting them the right to duty-free trade in lieu of a payment of Rs 3000 per year to the imperial treasury. They tried to use it for obtaining minting rights but this privilege was denied to them and the influence of the Jagat Seths was instrumental in this denial. The Seths had the monopoly of being the sole purchaser of bullion, and this was one more irritant to the English Company. Profssor Sushil Chaudhuri quotes from a letter of 1753 (only four years before the fatal quarrel of the Seths with Nawab Siraj-ud-Daula), written by the English factor of Kasimbazar, arguing that the setting up of a mint in Calcutta "could not be effected with the Nabab as it would be overset by Jagat Seat.... as he is a great gainer by being the sole purchaser of all Bullion imported."[23] The same difficulty was encountered by the French and the Dutch.[24] Here the principal obstacle to the Europeans was the price of bullion, which the Jagat Seths dictated by virtue of their unassailable position.

The Seths moreover received revenues from the *zamindars* on behalf of the Nawab's treasury. It might be described as some sort of a commercialization of state power, but as we shall see, this commercialization was only partial.

What needs to be emphasized here is that the bankers and *sarrafs* of pre-colonial Bengal did not hesitate to come into conflict with the Company whenever they felt their own needs were not served well enough. The story of their collaboration with Lord Clive in the latter's takeover of Bengal is well known. What is less known is that this collaboration in the political sphere notwithstanding, the money market remained an area of conflict. It was stated in a letter dated 29 September 1759, written by the Fort William authorities to the Court of Directors in London, "Our mint, (the mint in Calcutta) is at present of very little use to us as there has been no bullion sent out of Europe this season or two past, and we are apprehensive that it will never be attended with all the advantages we might have expected from it as the coming of *siccas* in Calcutta interfere so much with the interest of the Seats they will not fail of throwing every obstacle in our way to depreciate the value of our money in the country, notwithstanding its weight and standard is in every respect as good as the *siccas* of Murshidabad, so that a loss of *batta* will always arise in our money let our influence at the Durbar be ever so great." (italics added)[25] Again, there is a letter from the Court of Directors dated 17 March 1761 stating," We flatter ourselves if you give a due attention to see that the rupees coined in your mint are carefully and strictly kept up to the proper standard in weight and fineness they will pass currently notwithstanding your apprehensions of the Seats throwing obstacles in the way to depreciate their value on account as you intimate of its interfering with their interest. As this is an object we have long had our eyes upon, we shall depend upon your using every means in your powers to promote a free and extensive circulation of the money coined at Fort William as otherwise the grant for this priviledge will be of little use, and your present we doubt not will affect it."[26]

The Jagat Seths were the most successful bankers of pre-colonial Bengal and also of India, but their occasional intercession on behalf of the English and participation in the conspiracy against the Nawab in 1757 notwithstanding, they and the likes of them cannot truly be called the foundation of the English colonial regime in Bengal.

What was the measure of the *sarrafs'* involvement in Bengal's politics? The example of the Jagat Seths seems to suggest that it was considerable. But participation by the Seths cannot be generalized. The outcome of courtly politics might fatten those involved in it, or alternatively destroy them. Although the downfall of the Seths ironically began with Plassey, because they were hoist with their own petard and the situation boomeranged for them, the *sarrafs* and bankers functioning in relatively distant towns escaped this fate in general. At least they were not immediate victims of palace intrigues. This suggests that their involvement in courtly politics was insignificant, if it had existed at all.

From the foregoing, it should be clear that although the English East India Company, itself a commercial power, was dependent on native *sarrafs* and bankers in various degrees, it considered them as only a necessary evil, and after the assumption of the *diwani* (revenue administration of Bengal) in 1765, they were determined to eliminate the *sarrafs* as a class of surplus appropriators. It is ironical that their biggest collaborator in the final quarrel with Nawab Siraj-ud-Daula, namely the Jagat Seths, was the first to receive the immediate blow from the Company. After the victory in the Battle of Plassey, the Company began to make their purchases with the huge war indemnities received from the new Nawab, and no longer needed the service of the Murshidabad mint controlled by the Seths. This meant a large loss of mint income. The position of the English was further consolidated in consequence of the assumption of the *diwani.* The humiliation at the hands of Nawab Mir Kasim, who put two members of the family to death, was another blow to this banking house. The removal of the treasury from Murshidabad to Calcutta in 1773 and the closing of the Murshidabad mint in 1777 wiped out whatever official poer and privilege they had been enjoying.[27] About the same time, the General Bank for Bengal and Bihar was set up under the patronage of the Company's Government. The Jagat Seths continued to remain in business, although their fall from the zenith of prosperity was now decisive. Other bankers of Murshidabad too were grievously hurt owing to the formation of the General Bank. But the money market remained an area of conflict because the lesser *sarrafs* and bankers, particularly those operating in relatively distant areas, could not be suppressed so easily, although the Company sought to destroy their hold.

One source of strength of the *sarrafs* was the multiplicity of rupee coins in circulation and the *sarrafs* were not ready to yield to the writ of the Company's government in this matter. The struggle of the Patna *sarrafs* with the Company is a fine illustration of this struggle. The Patna mint was closed down in 1773 and the Government declared that it would receive only *sicca* rupees. The bankers of Patna bought up large stocks of *sicca* rupees and exchanged them for other kinds of rupee coins at excessively high rates of exchange. In 1780, when the administration, in order to put an end to their speculation in Patna *siccas*, reduced their value to that of *sonauts*, the bankers reacted by upgrading the value of *sonauts*. The Government tried to impose its writ over them, and they reacted by refusing to grant bills of exchange to the Government and foced the latter to seek a compromise. In more distant places, the control of the indigenous *sarrafs* remained strong enough, owing to their entrenched position in the rural economy and the relative lack of access of new financial institutions to these regions.[28]

In Bengal proper also, the indigenous *sarrafs* managed to frustrate many attempts of the Company at currecny reform. The monetary experiments of the Company have been narrated by two distinguished students of economic history, namely J.C. Sinha and N.K. Sinha, and later described in some detail by Debendra Bijay Mitra. The Company sought frantically to impose a uniform currency order. But the success was only partial. The first reform experiment of Clive, the first Governor-General, in 1766 sought to impose some sort of bimetallism with gold *muhrs* and silver rupees. One important feature of this bimetallism was the fixation of a mint ratio. The English Company, unlike the Mughal emperors, was itself a commercial power and its own mercantile interests could not allow it to leave the relative prices of gold *muhrs* and silver rupees to the vagaries of the market that were very much in existence. Rather, the Company wanted to have control over the market through its monetary reforms. In clive's monetary reform, the value of one gold *muhr* was to be 14 *sicca* rupees. But the ratio of the intrinsic worth of these two currencies in terms of market prices was about 1 : 11.5 Clive wanted to draw to the mint the hidden gold lying with the people in Bengal. But the Company recknoed without the host. The outcome of the experiment was that the divergence between the mint ratio and market ratio in the price of gold and silver led to the disppearance of silver from circulation and high discounts on gold coins.[29] The role of the *sarrafs* is clear. They did not want to cooperate with the Company's government in bringing the market ratio to the level of the mint ratio, because that would hurt their money-changing business. They instead created an artificial scarcity of silver coins so as to frustrate the intention of the government. So, the experiment turned into a fiasco. In short, the first battle between the Bangal *sarrafs* as money-changers and the Company ended—with a victory for the former. A not much different fate fell on Verselet's reform of 1769 for a similar reason. Here too the Government overvalued gold.[30] When Warren Hastings introduced his reform in 1777, by which it was decided to strike only the current *sicca* rupees, it was found that these rupees were not acceptable everywhere and they passed only at a high discount at *aurangs* (specialized weaving zones) from which the Company's residents used to procure their stocks of textiles. Besides, the *sarrafs* bought up all the Calcutta *siccas* and made it difficult for *zamindars* to pay revenue in this rupee, which was the only one acceptable to the Government. Other kinds of rupees continued to circulate in the interior.[31] In a letter dated 19 January 1783, it was reported by the commercial resident of

Rungpur that advances in *siccas* were unacceptable to *pykars* and agents as French *Arcots* were the most popular currency there. Here *Arcot* rupees accumulated in the hands of *sarrafs* claimed a premium. In a letter of 18 August 1784, it was reported that *saraafs* charged 100.6 *sicca* rupees for 100 *Arcots* in Dacca, where *Arcot* rupees were required to procure goods.[32] Such examples can be multiplied. What stands out is that *sarrafs* were not prepared to give up their entrenched position in the pluralistic money market.

The reform introduced by Lord Cornwallis in 1791 and expedited subsequently did not prove much of a success either. He declared the 19th sun *sicca* rupee to be the only currency. Since weavers in some *aurungs* had been used to other kinds of rupees, the new rupees were not acceptable to them. The *sarrafs* used the situation to depreciate the *sicca* rupee. The final data of official demonetization of other rupees had to be deferred. In order to alleviate the scarcity of coints, gold *muhrs* were also introduced; these coins and their fractional pieces were too high-valued for many transactions. Here too the *sarrafs* and bankers refused to release silver in exchange of gold. Again, gold *muhrs* in relation to silver rupees claimed a premium in the market probably because of the under-valuation of gold by the government.[33] The *sarrafs* were determined to take advantage of this under-valuation to their advantage.

In the extremely brief account outlined above, one might discover an attempt to telescope a long history into a few pages. But what should be clear from this sketchy description is that the intermediate-level *sarrafs* of Bengal, who were not as wealthy as to get involved in the politics of *durbar*, and yet had enough power to control the money markets of areas distant from Calcutta, provided a tough opposition to the Company's effort to secure hegemony in the monetary sphere. It is conceivable that a general situation of currency scarcity helped them to some extent. In Patna, wealthy bankers put up a serious challenge. In Bengal the struggle was by mofussil *sarrafs*, who had a firm grip over the money market in the interior, a grip they were not prepared to lose. They continued their fight. In the end, however, they were bound to lose the battle with the slow penetration of European-style banking institutions, backed by the might of the Government. How long these *sarrafs* survived and when the air of the unification of currency was realized cannot be said with certainty. But there is no doubt that the *sarrafs'* struggle for survival as an indigenous class lasted quite long. The Company rupee was introduced throughout the Company's territory in 1835, but it is not certain whether Bengal *sarrafs'* battle had been lost by then. There is definite evidence that in territories outside Bengal, the multiplicity of coins in circulation continued.[34]

The multiplicity of currencies in circulation was not a feature unique to Bengal. In upper India, this was very much in existence, and as the Company's rule expanded to this area, this represented a disorder from the new rulers' point of view. For instance, during 1828-31, it was reported from the divisions of Sahabad, Tirhut and Saran that the *ryots* were made to pay a *batta* owing to the lack of uniformity of coins, and Lord William Bentinck, the then Governor General, recommended the introduction of Farukabad rupees as the uniform currency. Bentinck grudgingly wrote, "Nothing indeed can well be more impolitic than to maintain between districts belonging to the same government and divided from each other by an arbitrary line only, a distinction in the currency which must seriously impeded their commercial intercourse."[35] Much earlier, Francis Buchanan (Buchanan Hamilton) had noted in course of his survey of the Shahabad district, "Although the revenue must be paid into the Collector's office in the *Kuldar* rupee coined at Calcutta not above a half of the silver currency is of that species... Most of the rents are under the management of moneylenders who find it much more advantageous to have the *Banaras* rupee as the currency than the *Kuldar*, the former not being a legal tender of payment, and therefore liable to whatever deduction they please under the name of exchange."[36] This is one example of the limited nature of the success of the state in unifying the currency.

Of course, the colonizing state, along with the steps towards the unification of currency, was building up new instutions of credit and banking. The General Bank for Bengal and Bihar, floated in 1773 by Warren Hastings, the then Governor of Bengal, was the first attempt in this direction. According to Amiya Kumar Bagchi, the Bank had the following objectives: (a) to regularize the *batta* between different types of coins circulating in the Company's territory; (b) to regulate the internal rate of exchange for transfer of funds from one place to another; and (c) to limit the extreme seasonal variations of the supply of coin by persuading the Collectors to deposit revenue in the branch houses of the Bank and take out bills on the head office payable in *sicca* rupees at a fixed rate of *batta* and *hoondian* (internal rate of exchange).[37] It is easily observable that these functions wer roughly the same that the House of Jagat Seth had been performing for the Nawab of Bengal. It is also interesting that the managers of the General Bank were two Indian bankers, Hazari (Huzuri) Mal and Dayal Chand, and that of the two main offices of the bank, one was in Calcutta and the other in Murshidabad. The General Bank was wound up after a brief existence. The first really state-backed European-style bank with limited liability was the Bank of Bengal set up in 1809. The notes of the Bank of Bengal were in some places preferred by *zamindars* for paying their revenues.[38]

The character of the bankers that were in the service of the Company needs to be examined. The Company dispensed with the House of Jagat Seths not before long, and the reasons are not far to seek. Even after the conspiracy against the Nawab, to which this House was party, and his dethronement and murder, the Company, as we have noted, looked upon the House with suspicion, and it did not expect the House to act as its subordinate. The administrators of the Company wanted to get away from the controlling influence of the House rapidly. A leading historian, in his bid to minimize the role of the colonizing state in the change that followied, has remarked, "But other indigenous capitalists quickly filled their role, though now fronted by and subordinate to the vast system of British peculation and inland trade." The loose and slipshod use of the term 'capitalist' notwithstanding, the historian who has throughout tried to minimize the role of the colonizing state has had thus to concede that these people did not collaborate with the British on their own terms (one may note the use of the words' fronted by and subordinate'). A little later, he writes, "These were not simply creatures of the British".[39] But the question is whether the position of these people was the same as those of the Jagat Seths and other bankers, who collaborated with the English on their own terms and hence had to engage in occasional struggles with them. Persons like Huzuri Mal, one of the managers of the General Bank for Bengal and Bihar, had based their business exclusively in Calcutta, and the same was the case with a group of other lesser merchants and bankers.[40] They were servile dependents rather than partners on an equal footing; one might call them compradors. But this character does not apply uniformly to all categories of *sarrafs* and bankers. The struggle by the lesser *sarrafs* and bankers, who had closer links with the agararian economy, clearly drives home the point that not all indigenous bankers were collaborators of the British. They fought, but, faced with the might of the Government that was itself a monopoly commercial power, they finally lost. The introduction of the Company rupee in 1835, marked a decisive step on the part of the state to end the vantage position of the indigenous rupee-dealing *sarrafs*, but as yet they went on circumventing the official writ in various ways.[41] The *cowrie*-dealing *sarrafs* had been declining ever since the beginning of the process of the gradual demonetization of *cowrie.* We shall dwell on this process of demonetization at length in the following chapter.

NOTES AND REFERENCES

1. Subrahmanyam, Sanjay. Introduction to *Money and Market in India* 1100–1700. Ed. Idem, O.U.P., 1994 : 32–33.
2. Haider, Najaf. "The Monetary Basis of Credit and Banking Instruments in the Mughal Empire". In *Money and Credit in India.* Ed. Amiya Kumar Bagchi. Delhi : Tulika, 2002 : 68.
3. Tavernier, Jean-Baptiste. *Travels in India,* Vol. 2. New Delhi : Munshiram Manoharlal, 1995 : 24.
4. Moosvi, Shireen. "Gujarati Ports and Their Hinterlands". In *Ports and their Hinterlands in India,* 1700–1950. Ed. Indu Banga. Delhi :

Manohar, 1992 : 128–29.

5. Habib, Irfan. Ibid, reprinted in idem: *Essays in Indian History,* Delhi, 1995 : 226–227.
6. Chaudhuri, Sushil. "The Financing of Investment in Bengal, 1650–1720". *I.E.S.H.R.* 8, no. 2 (1971) : 126–27.
   Chaudhuri, K.N. *The Trading World of Asia and the English East India Company.* C.U.P., 1978 : 184–85.
7. Raychaudhuri, Tapan. "Inland Trade". *C.E.H.I.* 1, ... : 346.
8. Habib, Irfan. "The System of Bills of Exchange in the Mughal Empire". In *Essays in Medieval Indian Economic History.* Ed. Satish Chandra. New Delhi : Munshiram Manoharlal, 1987 : 210–11.
9. Ahmadi, Mirat-I. 410–11, quoted in Habib, "Monetary System and Prices", *C.E.H.I.* I, Ch. XII (1) : 363.
10. Prakash, Om. "On Coinage in Mughal India". *I.E.S.H.R.* 25, no. 3 (1988) : 485–86.
11. Dasgupta, Ashin. "Indian Merchants and Trade in the Indian Ocean, c. 1500–1750". *C.E.H.I.* 1, Ch. XIII (2) : 420.
12. Prakash, Om. "Foreign Merchants and Indian Mints in the Seventeenth and Early Eighteenth Century". In *The Imperial Monetary System of Mughal India,* Ed. J.F. Richards. O.U.P., 1987 : 174.
    Habib, Irfan. The System of Bills of Exchange, 217.
13. vide Foot note 37 of Ch. 3.
14. Introduction to Little, J.H. *House of Jagat Seth.* Calcutta Historical Society : 1961 : XVII.
15. Om Prakash has raised this debate with a fair degree of apparent reasonableness. Vide, "On Coinage in Mughal India". *I.E.S.H.R.* 25, no. 4 (1988) : 488 –89.
16. Chakrabarty, Mukundaram. Chandimangla, Ed. Sukumar Sen : Third print. New Delhi : Sahitya Academy, 1993 : 66–67.
17. For evidence of this continuity, Om Prakash: The Dutch East India Company.... 233–34.
18. Marshall, Peter. *East Indian Fortunes...,* 86.
19. Mohsin, K.M. *A Bengal District in Transition:* Murshidabad 1765–1793 : 118–120.
20. Datta, Rajat. *Society, Economy and the Market; Commercialization in Rural Bengal* 1760–1800. New Delhi : Manohar, 2000 : 189–90.
21. Chaudhuri, Sushil. "General Economic Condition under the Nawabs." In *History of Bangladesh,* Vol. 1 : Asiatic Society of Bangladesh, 1992 : 64.
22. Sen, Sudipta. *The Empire of Free Trade.* Philadelphia: Pensylvania University Press, 1998 : 60.

23. Chaudhuri, Sushil. "European Companies and the Export Trade of Bengal in the Eighteenth Century". In *History of Bangladesh.* Ed. Islam. ..... 196–77.
24. Chaudhuri, Sushil: *From Prosperity to Decline....,* 79.
25. Ibid, p. 84.
26. *Fort William India House Correspondence,* Vol 2, 444.
27. Ibid, Vol 3, 77.
28. Mohsin, K.M. Banking in Mughal Bengal. Ed. Sirajul Islam. *History of Bangladesh,* Vol. 1. 242–43.
29. Chatterjee, Kumkum. "Collaboration and Conflict; Bankers and the Early Colonial Rule in India, 1757–1813". *I.E.S.H.R.* 30, no. 3 (1993) : 304–309.
30. Mitra, Debendra Bijay. *Monetary System in the Bengal Presidency* 1757–1835. Kolkata: K.P. Bagchi, 1991 : 28–32.
31. Chakrabarty, Subhra. "Intransigent Shroffs and the East India Company's Currency reforms in Bengal, 1757–1800". *I.E.S.H.R.* 34, no. 1 (1997) : 79–81.
32. Sinha, N.K. *Economic History of Bengal.* Kolkata, 1961 : 62.
33. Mitra, Debendra Bihay. Monetary System in the Bengal Presidency, 38.
34. Mitra: Ibid, 45–47, Sinha: Ibid, 133–34.
    Chakrabarti: Intransigent Shroffs...., 84–86.
35. Mitra : Ibid. 60–61.
36. Bagchi, Amiya Kumar. "Money and Credit as Areas of Conflict: Mimeographed". *C.S.S.S.* (1982) : 7–8.
37. Letter No. 158. *The Correspondences of Lord William Cavendish Bentinck.* Ed. C.H. Phillips, O.U.P., 1987.
38. Buchanan: *An Account of the District of Shahabad in 1812–13,* 1986 edition, Delhi, 438.
39. Bagchi, Amiya Kumar. *Evolution of the State Bank of India,* Vol I. Part I, New Delhi: O.U.P., 1986 : 45–46.
40. Gupta, Ranjan. *Economic Life of a Bengal District,* Birbhum 1770–1857. Burdwan University, 1984 : 242.
41. Bayly, C.A. *Indian Society and the Making of the British Empire, New Cambridge History of India,* II.I., C.U.P., Orient Longman, 1988 : 53–54.
42. Sen, Sudipta. *The Empire of Free Trade ....,* 96–97.
43. For a brief description, vide Amiya Kumar Bagchi: Money and Credit... passim.

Chapter Six

The Characteristics, Circulation and Decline of the Cowrie Currency

Earlier, we have given some hints about the circulation of the *cowrie* in pre-colonial India in general and Bengal in particular. In Bangal, there is an old saying, *phelo kari makho tel* (lay down your *cowrie* and take what you want), implying the superiority of hard cash over credit. In this province, *cowrie* is still used during the winter season in the worship of Laxmi, the goddess of wealth. In the early 1960s, a huge two-part Bengali novel entitled *Kari Diye Kinlam* was very popular and subsequently became the subject of a film. References to dual terms like *taka kari* and *paisa kari* in the day-to-day speeches of ordinary Bengalis are common till date. These examples show that in Bengal, the *cowrie* currency was considered synonymous with money itself, and its memory lingers through the ages, although its circulation had no formal state sanction, in the sense that it had no state guarantee about its intrinsic worth.

This point leads to the question as to whether *cowrie* was a kind of commodity money or token money. The absence of any guarantee about its intrinsic worth and its relative abundance compared with gold and silver might lead someone to think that it was a kind of token money. At least one noted authority on Indian monetary history has mentioned it as a kind of token currency.[1] To judge this question in its proper context, we have to remind ourselves that the question of intrinsic worth or value of a currency is not inseparable from the market. The metallic contents of a gold *muhr* or *pagoda* or silver rupee had some market value; the stamps of the mint only suggested the amount of metals contained therein. *Cowrie* also had a market value and in this sense, an intrinsic worth. As an anonymous Dutchman wrote in 1747: "What we call money being arbitrary and its nature and value depending on a tacit convention betwixt men, these (*cowrie*) shells, in several parts of Asia and Africa, are accounted current money with a value assigned to them. This is assigned by a reciprocal consent, and those who show a contempt of them don't reflect that these shells are as fit for a common standard of pecuniary value either as gold or silver."[2] This apt and well thought-out remark suggests that the *cowrie* was commodity money par excellence. It was commodity money, but not King's money or merchants' money. It was people's money although merchants and sometimes even kings used it for setting their transactions. The fact of dominance of this kind of money in some regions should go a long way in demolishing the so-called forced commercialization theory.

Another interesting point that reinforces our conclusion is that the demand and supply of *cowrie* were not constrained by any royal convention. At the port of Hooghly, the English found to their dismay that Murshidabad rupees were more in demand than Surat and Patna rupees, in spite of being of the same weight and finesse, and hence fetched a higher market price. Hooghly was a port of Bengal and the coin bearing the stamp of the Nawab of Bengal commanded a premium there. Such elements were naturally absent in the determination of the market price of the *cowrie.* Surat and Patna were more distant from Hooghly than Murshidabad, the capital of the province, and the price of a silver rupee varied inversely with the distance between the place of production and place of circulation. For *cowrie,* a reverse situation seemed to exist. In the 1660s, Tavernier, the French jeweller then travelling in India, noted, "Close to the sea up to 80 are given for the *paisa,* but the number diminishes as you leave the sea, on account of the cost of carriages; so that at Agra you receive but 50 or 55 rupees for the *paisa.*"[3] What is implied here is that the supply of *cowrie* was plentiful in regions close to the sea relative to the demand. In the interior, supply was not as abundant. There was, however, no additional factor like the name of a king or nawab influencing the demand. Hence the process of determination of the market price of *cowrie* was more objective than that of silver rupees in the economic sense.

Another point concerning the intrinsic value of *cowrie* is that no monetary substance can command an intrinsic market value unless it has some other uses and a supply that is not unlimited like air or water. *Cowrie* had also some alternative uses. In Bengal as well as West Africa, *cowrie* was used as ornaments and toys, and for ceremonial purposes. In Portuguese ships it was used as ballasts. It is interesting that the use of *cowrie* as money and ornaments propelled the Portuguese to use it as ballasts as against stones, sands and old rusted iron, because the former could fetch them some earnings, while the latter could not.

A commodity currency that could not be clipped or fabricated should have served at least partly as a medium of exchange in the international sphere. Recent research has revealed the fact of the fairly widespread circulation of *cowrie* in West Africa. Vigorous *cowrie* markets developed in important European cities such as London, Lisbon, Hamburg and Amsterdam in the 17th-18th centuries. Amsterdam had the largest *cowrie* market and the chief supplier was the Dutch East India Company. Over time, the Dutch wrested control of the European *cowrie* trade from the Portuguese.[4] The principal buyers of *cowrie* in the European market were the European Companies such as the English Royal African Company, and private merchants engaged in trade with Africa. *Cowrie* was taken to West Africa by sea route or across the Saharan desert on the back of camels and donkeys. According to one authority, about 400 million *cowries* were annually imported into West Africa in the early 18th century.[5] The pricipal items of exchange were salves and palm oil. *Cowrie* was shipped to East Africa as well, but its use there was probably not very significant.[6] The importance of African slave trade to the capital accumulation process of the Europeans is well documented[7] and the export of *cowrie* to West Africa was a necessary instrument of this process. There is no evidence, however, of the circulation of *cowrie* as a currency medium anywhere in Europe. Another important *cowrie*-using region was the province of Yunnan in China. In Yunnan, the *cowrie* served not only as a medium of exchange but also as a means of tax payment.[8]

Now let us turn to the Indian subcontinent. In our discussion on inflation in Mughal India, we have argued that the evidence of the rise of copper prices suggests that *cowrie* replaced copper partly as a currency medium in the wake of the appreciation of copper prices in the 17th century. Probably *cowrie* continued to remain in circulation along with copper coins in Mughal India, because we do not have any evidence that copper returned as a major currency metal towards the end of the 17th century, at least as far as the Mughal imperial mints were concerned. *Cowrie* was in use in western Deccan as well. In Bombay Presidency, the English found, along with a large number of gold, copper and silver coins, *cowrie* in circulation.[9] It is interesting that in south India, there is no evidence of the circulation of *cowrie* in ordinary acts of purchase and sale, although exports of rice from Malabar to the Maldives was considerable, and the Moplah merchants had a vigorous participation in *cowrie* trade in the coastal areas of Bengal and Orissa. In Bengal (and Orissa), the importance of *cowrie* remained overwhelming because there was no copper mint. It is quite probable that the Mughals did not try to disturb the tradition of *cowrie* use. Before the Mughal period, *cowries* were exchanged with silver coins of the Afgan era. On the reference to the *tanka* made by the poet of *Chandimangal* (vide Chapter 5), it should be remembered that "no Mughal coinage of Bengal provenance is known prior to AH 1002 (1593-4)".[10] In the same poetic work, *ganda, pan* and *kahan* are mentioned as units of counting *cowries*.

One *ganda* = 4 pieces
One *pan* = 80 pieces
One *kahan* = 1,280 pieces

The prevalence of *cowrie* in the Mughal period in low-value transactions in Bengal highlights the failure of the Mughals to introduce the system of trimetallism in this province. One definite reason is the low prices of foodstuffs and other necessities, which allowed *cowrie* to remain the dominant currency in low-value transactions. A second reason might be surmised. In Bengal, the imperial system of administration based on *mansabdars* was rather weak and the local potentates of the countryside called *zamindars* enjoyed a much larger share of power than in the Mughal core regions. This relative autonomy perhaps was one of the factors preventing a full-scale Mughal hegemony in the monetary sphere.

A few lines are necessary on the identity of traders importing *cowrie* into Bengal. In the 16th century, the Portuguese began to bring stocks of *cowrie* to Bengal. According to one calculation, there were 300 to 400 per cent differences in the price of the *cowrie* as between the Maldives and Bengal.[11] Among the Indian traders, the Moplah merchants operating from the Malabar coast dominated the *cowrie* trade with Bengal at least till the first half of the 17th century.[12] Thereafter, Bengal merchants began to participate directly in this trade. In an earlier chapter, we have referred to the participation of Mughal officials in Bengal's sea-borne trade. After the withdrawal of these officials in the late 17th century, the sea-borne trade of merchants stationed in Bengal became confined to voyages to the Maldives and to import of *cowrie*.[13] There is definite evidence of participation of English merchants as well as the English East India Company in the *cowrie* trade.[14] It should be mentioned that although the English used to bring *cowrie* to Bengal, a part of the stock was directed to Europe via the port of Chittagong. From a correspondence between the Fort William (the Calcutta office of the English East India Company) and the India House (the headquarters of the Company in London), it appears that there might have existed some sort of ambivalence regarding whether to bring the *cowrie* into Bengal or to send it to the European market.[15] It is curious that the Dutch East India Company, which reportedly tried to secure a monopoly of the *cowrie* trade in Europe, did not bring any *cowrie* to Bengal, although they made brisk business in Bengal's mechandise and brought huge stocks of Japanese copper regularly.[16] The only possible explanation for this phenomenon might be that the Dutch had such a large market for *cowrie* in Europe that they did not have any excess supply with which to feed Bangal's growing demand.

Another point regarding *cowrie* is its acceptance in revenue payment. English merchants witnessed this in 1750. There are reports of revenue payment in *cowrie* in the early period of the Company's revenue administration.[17] Here it should be remembered that the primary currency for the fixation of revenue was the rupee (and its fractional piece, *anna*) and not *cowrie*. *Cowrie*, however, entered into calculation of revenue as well as the payment and realization of advances (*dadans*) in the absence of the copper pice. The net balance of the Council of Revenue in Murshidabad, according to the settlement of 1771, is shown to be 18 lakh, 38 thousand and 661 rupees.[18] In 1804, the Fort William authorities were asking the Collectors to receive revenue at the rate of 5,280 *cowries* for one silver rupee.[19] From the account books of a leading business family of the district of Birbhum, namely the Sarkars of Surul, it is learnt that they used to pay advances in rupees, *annas* and *cowrie* (calculated in *gandas*) even in the closing years (1796-97) of the 18th century.[20] The circulation of *cowrie* on such a scale again suggest that it is difficult to accept the hypothesis of monetization forced by revenue payment. The amount of revenue was estimated primarily in terms of *sicca* rupees, not *cowrie*. So, if revenue collected from one unit is liable to be converted into rupees and *annas*, there is no reason why *cowrie* should circulate on such a scale, necessitating regular imports of this monetary medium.

From the foregoing discussion, it should be clear that the decline of *cowrie* and its eventual disappearance from circulation was an important aspect of monetary transition in Bengal in the early colonial times. It will follow from the very sequel that the transition was prmarily due to a number of economic factors, supplemented and backed by the colonizing process initiated by the English East India Company. The upshot of the colonization process was, however, more far-reaching than the decline of *cowrie*. Nevertheless, the decline was a historically important and analytically interesting episode.

A fact to be noted is that in the late pre-colonial economy of Bengal, i.e. in the economy of Bengal in the first half of the 18th century, there was a relative stability of *cowrie* prices of rupees, along with stability in the rupee prices of goods. This is because, along with large inflows of rupees, there were parallel inflows of *cowrie* from the Maldives to lubricate the growing monetary economy of Bengal. From this, it can be easily conjectured that there was stability in the *cowrie* prices of goods. In short, the tradition of *cowrie* use survived because the economy supported it.

This age-old status quo began to crack in the wake of the Battle of Plassey in 1757, leading to the dethronement and killing of Nawab Siraj-ud-Daula. In respect of the currency situation, this resulted in the cessation of imports of silver by the English East India Company. The English company received large amounts of money as war indemnities and gifts, which came in handy for them. After the assumption of the revenue-administration (*diwani*) of Bengal in 1765, there was no further need for bringing in imports, because the Company could, from then on, finance its purchases (investments) out of the revenue of Bengal. More important, other European Companies too stopped their imports of silver almost entirely. The reason for this phenomenon is interesting. The European servants of the English company amassed huge wealth by means of trade in Bengal's goods, but they could not declare this income owing to legal prohibitions. Hence they resorted to the trick of depositing this ill-gotten wealth with other European Companies, particularly the Danes and the Dutch, in lieu of bills of exchange that were payable in Europe. As one authority puts it succinctly, "The Dutch, the Danes and the French all acted clandestinely as agents for private British traders and the Company's servants. There was widespread evasion of restrictions on British private trade in the whole period up to 1793, and this evasion continued thereafter although on a slightly diminished scale."[21] The remittance of bills under the Danish flag was particularly important. The directors of the Danish Company in Copenhagen stopped sending silver to India in 1775, and more than half of the return cargoes were financed through "such Anglo-Indian remittance capital against bills on the (Danish) Asiatic Company."[22] In the most authentic study of the subject, it has been remarked, "Illicit Anglo-India remittance and trade was an absolute condition for the existence of a private trade between India and Copenhagen. Only a continued conflict of itnerest between the English Company on one side and on the other, its Anglo-Indian servants and the growing British Anglo-Indian commercial interests, could maintain a lucrative transit trade on foreign account through Copenhagen. Risk and profit, therefore fell primarily to the Anglo-Indians, but the Danish proxies in India, the Copenhagen merchant houses and Danish Government drew large, unearned incomes from the traffic."[23]

The year 1793 was significant in the sense that in the Company's charter of this year, private traders were granted the right to use 3000 tonnes of the Company shipping space at lower freight rates. The objective was to check the scale of evasion.[24] But there was no reason to think that this diminsished the outflow of silver. The combined result of these was the creation of a server shortage of the rupee currency.

Three other factors should be noted in explaining the scarcity of silver. One was the Company's trade with China. Transport of silver to China on account of this trade began in 1757 and continued uninterrupted till 1770. Thereafter money continued to be remitted to China on private accounts, but this did not indicate any change in the outflow of silver currency.[25] Another factor contributing to the silver scarcity was the need to finance the Company's expansionary wars of conquest, i.e. the Anglo-Mysorean war and the Anglo-Maratha war. A fourth factor was the investment of money in diamond trade by the Company's officials and the consequent drainage of silver to Oudh and Hyderabad.[26] The severity of the crisis of the rupee currency can be guessed from one incident of 1794 in the district of Birbhum of southern Bengal. The District Judge wrote to the Collector that since the monthly salary of many of the employees of his court was less than one *muhr* each, arrangements should be made to pay the salaries in rupees. The Collector in reply only pleaded his helplessness.[27]

On the scarcity of the silver currency, there is, however, a different opinion that should be considered. In a recent study,

Professor Rajat Datta has argued that there were bullion crises in 1722 and 1729, and compared with 1729, the monthly rates of *batta* on *sicca* rupees in relation to *Arcot* rupees were lower during 1769-1773. Professor Datta argues that since bullion was imported by the English Company to be coined into *sicca* rupees, the lower *batta* rates show that "notions of a great scarcity of silver and silver currency are difficult to sustain."[28]

The question is how far the rate of *batta* is a reliable yardstick in estimating the abundance or scarcity of a particular currency. In the 1760s, *Arcot* rupees were very much in circulation in Bengal, and a somewhat lower rate of *batta* on *sicca* rupees might indicate a scarcity of the former in relation to the latter, compared with 1729. But this is not sufficient to negate the notion of a general scarcity of silver currency. It is true that the investments of the English Company went up phenomenally after its assumption of *diwani*, and it is possible that the revenues it could set aside for investment were not sufficient. But that does not explain the entire picture. In particular, we have to consider the phenomenon of clandestine trade, which almost certainly had a depressing effect upon the inflow of bullion into Bengal.

When a particular currency becomes scarce, it is natural that its price in terms of other currencies should go up. This is exactly what happened in this period. In the pioneering essay of Sushil Chandra De, it is reported that the price of one rupee was 2400 *cowries* in 1740. But it went up to 4000 to 5200 in 1771.[29] According to C.R. Wilson, the quoted price of a silver rupee in *cowrie* at the Fort William was 2560 in 1703.[30] Again, "by a proclamation dated 10th October, 1804, the collectors were asked to accept revenue in *sicca* rupees and failing that, in *cowries*, the rate of exchange being 4 *kahans* and 12 *pans* or 5240 pieces for one Calcutta *sicca* rupee."[31] This shows that the price of *cowrie* was falling rapidly. Whatever the correctness of Professor Datta's estimates, it may be admitted that the supply of silver currencies was not so plentiful as to arrest the downward trend in the rupee prices of *cowrie*.

Yet it should be noted that the downward trend in the rupee price of *cowrie* was not smooth and spatially uniform. For example, in the wake of the demonetization in 1792 of all other currencies except the 19th sun *sicca* rupee by Lord Cornwallis, the then Governor General, the *cowrie* price of the rupee went down in some weaving areas. The weavers demanded *cowries*, but were paid in *muhrs* and *sicca* rupees.[32] Such localized fluctuations, however, do not disprove the fact of a declining trend in the price of *cowrie*.

Yet the decline in the rupee price of *cowrie* could hardly be a valid ground for its disappearance from circulation. Many of the *cowrie*-using people seldom used rupee currencies in their day-to-day business of life. Holden Furber, the celebrated historian of Company trading, made a highly perceptible remark, "Because few of those who used *cowrie* extensively ever saw more than one rupee at a time or moved out of the region where they were born, the value of the local *cowrie* in terms of silver did not greatly matter."[33] It follows that what really mattered was not the *cowrie* price of rupees, but the cowrie price of goods. There is practically no recorded evidence on the *cowrie* price of goods. As the second-best solution, we can try to see the trend in the rupee prices of goods and then make a conjecture, because if rupee prices of goods rose, so must the cowrie prices of the same if the rupee prices of cowries were on the decline.

There are hopefully some findings on the price of consumption goods. One important consumption item was salt. Even during the disturbing periods of Nawab Alibardi Khan, i.e. the 1740s, the price of salt was forty, fifty or sixty rupees per 100 *maunds*[34] (one *maund* is equivalent to 37.5 kg). In 1772, the Company's Government assumed full control over the salt trade. In 1773, the price was Rs 170 per 100 *maunds*. In 1778, the price varied between Rs 312 and Rs 409 per 100 *maunds*. In 1790 the same price was between Rs 234 to Rs 314. In 1798 the range of salt prices was between Rs 306 and Rs 380 per 100 *maunds*. And in 1803-04 the price was Rs 342, on an average.[35] This was merely one aspect of the inflationary situation. Information regarding the price movements of other essential commodities can be had from Hameeda Hossian's work.

The price of rice rose substantially between 1754 and 1793, amidst fluctuations. The price of sugar rose, but not very prominently. The price of mustard oil rose substantially, although in a fluctuating manner. The price of clarified butter also rose substantially.[36] These findings only bear testimony to the presence of general inflationary situation in Bengal. It is curious that this inflationary situation showed up when there was an outflow of ruppes from Bengal, which proves that attempts to relate price rise to money supply are not always worthwhile. En passant, it may be metioned that all these prices were quoted in rupees.

We can now digress a little, and refer to some earlier writings on the subject. Some historians, notably K.K. Datta, Brajen Gupta, K.N. Chaudhuri and Peter Marshall had argued the case for a price rise in Bengal in the late pre-colonial period. But Sushill Chauduri, drawing attention to the unreliable nature of the sources and the necessity of distinguishing between various types under one head of commodities, has persuasively shown that this might not have been the case. His views have been discussed earlier. But Sushil Chaudhuri has also not disputed the evidence of price rise in the post-Plassey situation. So, there seems to be a consensus that there was a significant price rise in the post-Plassey period.

It should be clear that this price rise in terms of rupees implies a similar rise in terms of *cowries* also, and, considering that the rupee prices of the *cowrie* were falling, the price rise in terms of *cowries* must have been sharper.

Now the reasons for this price rise need a little exploration, because they seemingly have a bearing on the issue of decline of the *cowrie* currency. K.N. Chaudhuri has referred to the large rise in 'investments' (purchases) of the English East India Company and consequent probable inflationary pressure. Peter Marshall has explicitly argued that this was responsible for the price rise.[37] But they have not been able to demonstrate convincingly that total aggregate effective demand rose significantly. How far the rise in the 'investment' of the English Company took place at the expense of their European rivals and Asian merchants is also a moot question.

There were other changes in the economy. One of these was the large increase in nominal revenue demand. R.C. Dutt has noted in his *Economic History of India Under the Early British Rule* : "The last Mahammadan ruler of Bengal, in the last year of his administration (1764) realized a land revenue of 817,533 pounds; within thirty years, the British rulers realized a land revenue of 2680000 pounds in the same province."[38] The repressive character of revenue demands, it may be mentioned, had been noted much earlier by the Company's administrators, and both Warren Hastings and Phillip Francis, the two Company officials famous for their mutual hostility, were of the opinion that high taxation compelled *ryots* and manufacturers to raise the prices of necessities of life.[39]

With the help of a simple algebraic model, we may try to link phenomena like the increase in the *cowrie* prices of the rupee, rise in the rupee prices of goods, the increased revenue burden and the monopolistic position of the Company in the trade of some items like salt with the process of decline of *cowrie.* It should be noted at the outset that the revenue was assessed in rupees, not *cowries.*

Let us assume a two-commodity model, X_1 and X_2 being the respective amounts of the two commodities produced. Let the total amount of revenue to be paid be R (in rupees), and P_1 and P_2 be the *cowrie* prices of these two commodities. Again, let a and b be the proprtions of the two commodities sold for making revenue payment, If Prc is the *cowrie* price of the rupee, the basic equation of the model is

$$P_1 aX_1 + P_2 bX_2/\mathrm{Prc} = R$$

Now, when R rises, producers or their representatives have to raise either P_1 or P_2 or both. Alternatively, they can raise *a* or *b* or both. According to colonial administrators like Francis and Hastings, the former happened to be the case in the seventies of the 18th century. In this case, the usefulness of *cowrie,* already an extremely low-priced currency, as a medium of exchange must go down. If Prc rises, this usefulness is further diminished, because then the *cowrie* prices of goods have to be raised further in order to meet revenue obligations. In the case of goods like salt or raw silk, where the Company itself appeared on the scene as a monopsonistic purchaser, the scope of raising these prices was bound to be much more circumscribed; the producers in such cases would have little option but to raise *a* and *b*. This is turn implies a contraction of the *cowrie*-using horizontal exchange economy, which again is reinforced by the rise in Prc. The impact of the increased revenue demand might be lessened if *d* Prc > *d*R, which was out of question in this case because *d*Prc was clearly less than zero.

Yet the final decline and disappearance of *cowrie* as a medium of exchange had to await the introduction of another low-priced—but not as low-priced as the depreciated cowire—currency medium. The Company's Government brought out this medium in the shape of the copper pice and half pice. The first copper coins were presumably introduced in the 1780s with indigenous copper. But then the Court of Directors took the responsibility upon itself. Its keenness in this regard can be understood from one incident. In 1790, the Court of Directors purchased copper coins worth 4000 pound-sterlings from England's Messrs Boulton and Watt. In 1793, this purchase was doubled.[40] Quite naturally, *cowrie* was then in retreat. Later, still smaller currencies like *pai* (one-third of a pice) and *chhidam* (one-fourth of a pice) were introduced to hasten the retreat.

One standard opinion regarding the decline of *cowrie* is that the Company's government, by a Regulation of 1807, refused to accept *cowrie* in revenue payment and thereafter the demand for and price of *cowrie* fell precipitously.[41] A similar opinion ('switch in the means of tax payment') has been expressed by Hans Ulrich Volgel in explaining the decline of *cowrie* in Yunnan. Vogel also informs us that after some previous unseccuessful attempts, copper coins (cash) began to be minted at a lower cost by 1650 and in this year official prohibition was imposed on *cowrie.*[42] Here too a combination of administrative fiat and introduction of an officially sponsored coin supposedly played the trick. It is beyond our competence to examine the veracity of Vogel's conclusion. But a careful scrutiny of the evidence obtainable on the monetary situation in the first phase of the colonian rule in Bengal seems to suggest a serious qualification of such a notion. As we have seen, the price of *cowrie* in terms of rupees began to fall before 1807. Besides, the price of goods also began to rise in Bengal, which had been relatively unaffected by inflationary pulls in the pre-colonial period. Moreover, *cowrie* was not the only currency used in revenue payment, nor was its use confined to revenue payment only. One example may be given to illustrate the point. In the district of Birbhum, *zamindars* were seen paying revenue in gold, not in *cowrie,* in the last two decades of the 18th century.[43] So, it would be wrong to attibute to the regulation of 1807 such a pivotal role in the decline of *cowrie.* Of course, in regions where payment of revenue in *cowrie* had been standard practice, the impact of the Regulation was conceivably much more acute. The rate of exchange in Orissa was 5120 (four *kahans*) *cowries* to a *sicca* rupee in 1803. In 1833, the rate went down to 8 to 9 *kahans.* Such a fall was at least partially the outcome of the Regulation of 1807.[44] In this sense, the Regulation expedited the decline.

In her study of the *cowrie*-using economy of West Africa, Marian Johnson has argued that with the increasing export-orientation of the West African economy, imports of goods in exchange of palm oil replaced imports of *cowrie* and other products and in this process, the role of *cowrie* was to serve as a nuit of account. The result, Johnson has argued, was contraction of *cowrie*-using internal economy.[45] Comparing the West African situation with the Bengal scenario, one difference can hardly be missed. One far-reaching change that took place in the *cowrie*-using economy of the Bengal countryside was the drainage of vast quantities of goods in consequence of the demand for and realization of exorbitant amounts of revenue. This can be considered as one kind of unrequited export.

The fall in the price of *cowrie* affected the *cowrie*-dealing *sarrafs* (*potdars*) severely, because they had to suffer considerable capital losses. Whether the fall in price led them to release larger stocks of *cowrie* in anticipation of further losses, and thus to accelerate the fall, is a matter of curiosity, but we have no evidence against which such a hypothesis can be tested.

Whether the replacement of *cowrie* by the Company's copper coin relieved the shortage of suitable currency media may be a point worthy of discussion. From whatever information we have at our disposal, it seems that at least for some periods and some regions, the number of copper coins was not enough and there took place some sort of demonetization. Francis Buchanan (Buchanan Hamilton) found in Patna and the adjacent areas a scarcity of copper coins and a higher rupee-pice ratio than the mint ratio in 1811-12. Buchanan noted that persons who took copper pices at the official rate of 64 per rupee were getting a good margin of profit, as the market rate varied from 54 to 58. The same dearth of the Company's copper coin and the widespread circulation of crude copper coins were observed in the district of Shahabad.[46] From Ranjan Gupta's study of Birbhum, a similar picture is found for almost the same period. Gupta has observed, "After the first decade of the (eighteenth) century, the monetary system tended to be normal through the increasing use of bank notes (notes of Bengal Bank being preferred) in Government transactions. But this progress, even if unsteady, occurred with regard only to the high-denomination currency. In regard to the small denomiantion coins, especially the coins of single pice and half-pice issued between 1796 and 1808, the dearth persisted. ...In 1814, gold and copper coins were 'scarcely procurable' in the district.... The poor people, while going from one place to another carried with them a large bundle of *cowries* to defray their travelling charges, to avoid so heavy a *batta* on smaller coins."[47] The situation was clearly one of near-demonetization. It was a period when the scarcity of rupee currencies had largely disappeared, thanks to imports of silver bullion by individual merchants as well as by the Government,[47] but there was a scarcity of copper coins. *Cowries* continued to circulate with a much-diminished value. The note issues of the Bank of Bengal, as this observation reveals, gave some sort of relief to *zamindars,* but these issues could not relieve the problem arising out of the shortage of low-denomination copper coins. But even then, these issues paved the way for the hoarding of relatively high-value coins and their fractional pieces. As has been put in the most authoritative study on the history of banking in India, "Earlier, the *zamindars* or merchants had to pay their dues to the government or other large creditors in specie and some of that trickled down to the ordinary people and met their needs for a universally acceptable medium of exchange. Under the new dispensation, the landlords or big merchants simply took bank notes and paid in bank notes, and the *hoondian* was generally small. They were now able to hoard any gold and silver that came their way, particularly in years when business was slack. This means that the common people had great difficulty in procuring a medium of exchange that would be acceptable to the government or for purchases from outside their villages or small towns."[48]

Buchanan found *cowries* in fairly widespread circulation in rural exchanges in Purnea.[49] We have already referred to the circulation of *cowrie* in Orissa in 1833. In Bastar, a region lying between Orissa and the Godavari belt, *cowrie* was found in circulation even in 1870, at the rate of 4032 *cowries* per rupee.[51] When the *cowrie* currency finally disappeared from circulation cannot be said with any degree of certainty, but there can be no doubt that there were considerable *inter*-temporal and inter-spatial variations in this regard.

It should be emphasized that the decline of *cowrie* took place in a phase of vigorous empire-building, launched by the colonizing state. Vogel, in his account of the disapperance of the *cowrie* from circulation in Yunnan, has expressed a similar opinion—we have not, however, shared his emphasis on administrative fiat in our analysis of the situation in Bengal—and here it was not any colonizing foreign power, but the Central Chinese Government that sought to impose a legitimacy of its rule over the frontier regions.[52] Such sort of empire-building might take place even under the jurisdiction of a capitalist government ruling over the home country when, with some structural change taking place in the economy, some hitherto important media of exchange and the institutions representing them might go out of the scene altogether. The widespread circulation of *cowrie* represented a dualistic monetary structure in Bengal. To give a historical analogy, the country banks that grew up in Britain during the Industrial Revolution represented the lower echelons of a similar dualistic structure. These banks, after fulfilling their historical mission, had to give way to the power of the joint-stock banks that began to open branches in the districts since the immediate aftermath of the Industrial Revolution. In the most authentic study of country banks in Britain, this process is characterized as a phase of "aggressive empire-building". The final disappearnce of these country banks took place in the 20th century.[53] In this process, the arms of the state were less visible (although not invisible) because in Britain, the so-called separation between the economic and political spheres had already been completed. The decline and disappearance of country banks, however, took place over an entire historical epoch, much similar to the decline and disappearance of *cowrie.* It signified a structural change in British capitalism, centralization of the production economy and of bank capital. In India too a new situation was emerging. With the rise of Britain as the leader of world capitalism, there emerged the era of the gold standard and the pound-sterling came to regarded 'as good as gold'. In this specific phase of 'globalization', the Indian monetary system had to play a servitor role. Here there was no place for indigenous currencies devised by the people. The *cowrie* currency, however, continued to survive in the vocabulary of the masses and in literature.

NOTES AND REFERENCES

1. Bagchi, Amiya Kumar. *Evolution of the State Bank of India,* Vol. 1, Part 1. New Delhi: O.U.P., 1986 : 22.
2. Cited in Marion Johnson : "The Cowrie Currencies of West Africa, Part 1". *Journal of African History.* 12, no. ...... (1970) : 17.
3. Tavernier, Jean-Baptiste. *Travels in India,* Vol. 1. New Delhi : Munshiram Manoharlal, 1995 : 22.
4. Glaman, Kristoff. "European Trade 1500–1750". In *The Fontana Economic History of Europe, The Sixteenth the Seventeenth Centuries.* Ed. Cipolla. 450–51, Jan Hogendron and Marion Johnson: Shell Money and Slave Trade, C.U.P., 1986 : 40.
5. Johnson, Marion. The Cowrie Currencies of West Africa...., 44.
6. Newitt, M.D.D. "East Africa and Indian Ocean Trade". In *India and the Indian Ocean, 1500–1800.* Eds. Ashin Dasgupta and M.N. Pearson. New Delhi: O.U.P., 1999 : 202.
7. For a lucid account, vide Amiya Kumar Bagchi: *The Political Economy of Underdevelopment,* Orient Longman, New Delhi 1989 : 43–48.
8. Hans Ulrich Vogel. "Cowry Trade and the Economy of Yunnan". *J.E.S.H.O.* 36, no. 2&3, ( ) : 211–252 and 309–353.

9. Fukazawa, H. "The State and the Economy, Maharastra and the Deccan". *C.E.H.I.* 1, Ch. VII (2) : 202.
10. Vide Footnote of Ch. 2.
11. Hogendron and Johnson. *Shell Money and Slave Trade*... 36.
12. Arasaratnam, S. "Ceylon in the Indian Ocean Trade". In *India and the Indian Ocean*..... Ed. Dasgupta and Pearson. New Delhi: O.U.P., 1999 : 102, 115.
13. Prakash, Om. *The Dutch East India Company and the Economy of Bengal, 1640–1730*. New Delhi: O.U.P., 1998 : 233–34. Ashin Dasgupta: Bangopasagar, Kolkata, 1989, p. 22, S. Arasaratnam: Maritime Trade in India in the Seventeenth Century. New Delhi: O.U.P., 1997 : 171.
14. Ray, Indrani. "India in Asian Trade in the 1730s". In *Essays in Honour of Prof. S.C. Sarkar*. Ed. Barun De. People's Publishing House, Delhi: 1976: 228–29.
    De, Sushil Chandra. "The Cowrie Currency of India". *Orissa Historical Journal*. 1, no. 1, (1952) : 7–8.
    Sen, Sudipta. *The Empire of Free Trade*. Philadelphia : Pensylvania University Press, 1998 : 78.
15. *Fort William-India House Correspondence,* Volume V. "The Assortment of cowries, sent from the Presidency of Fort St. Gorge on the Royal Admiral appearing from a Report of the Export warehouse keeper to be ill calculated for Europe Markets we have directed them to be disposed of at public outcry." p. 389. Holden Furber has given a piece of information suggesting that the Court of Directors was interested in procuring *cowries* through their Bombay Government for investment in slave trade even as late as 1789–93. Vide Furber: *John Company at Work*. Cambridge: Harvard University Press, 1948 : 289–90.
16. Prakash, Om: *The Dutch East India Company*.... Table 5.2.
17. Yule, Henry and A.C. Burness. *Hobson-Jobson: A Glossary of Anglo-Indian Words and Phrases and of Kindred Terms*. New Delhi: Munshiram Manoharlal, 1976 : 270. K.M. Mohsin: *A Bengal District in Transition, Murshdabad* 1765–1793. Dacca : Asiatic Society of Bangladesh, 1973 : 118. W.W. Hunter: *Annals of Rural Bengal*. Kolkata : Government of West Bengal, 1996 : 34, 285.
18. Hunter: Ibid, p. 285.
19. Mitra, Debendra Bijay. *Monetary System in the Bengal Presidency 1757–1835*. Kolkata : K.P. Bagchi, 1991 : 88.
20. Gupta, Ranjan. *Rahrer Samaj, Arthaniti O Gana Bidroha*. Kolkata: Subarnarekha, 2001 : 330.
21. Bagchi, Amiya Kumar. *Evolution of the State Bank*... 20.

22. Ole feldback; *India under the Danish Flag* 1772–1808. Student Litteratur, 1969 : 26–28.
23. Ibid : 238–39.
24. Bagchi, Amiya Kumar. *Evolution of the State Bank....*, 20.
25. Mitra, Debendra Bijay. *Monetary System in the Bengal Presidendy...* pp. 25–26, Bagchi: Ibid, 20–24.
26. Mitra, Ibid, p. 27, C.A. Bayly: *Rulers, Townsmen and Bazaars.* C.U.P., 1986, pp. 231–32. Furber: *John Company at work....* Ch. 1, 3–31 passim.
27. Gupta, Ranjan. *Economic Life of a Bengal District,* Birbhum 1770–1857. University of Burdwan, 1984 : 240–41.
28. Datta, Rajat. *Society, Economy and the Market, Commercialization in Rural Bengal* c1760–1800, 342–350.
29. De, Sushi Chandra. The Cowrie Currency...., 8–10.
30. Wilson, C.R. *The Early Annals of the English in Bengal,* Part 1. Reprint. Kolkata: Asiatic Society of Bengal, 1996, 219.
31. Vide Footnote 19.
32. Mitra. *Monetary System in the Bengal Presidency....* , 87–90.
33. Furber. John Company.... 287.
34. Sinha, N.K. Introduction to Salt Papers, Sinha : *The Historian as Archivist* (Selected papers of N.K. Sinha). Kolkata : 1997 : 146.
35. Sinha. Ibid, p. 150. Iftikar-ul-Awwal. "The State of Indigenous Industries". *The History of Bangladesh,* Vol. 1. Ed. Sirajul Islam. 338.
36. Hossain, Hameeda. *The Company Weavers of Bengal; The East India Company and the Organization of Textile Production in Bengal* 1750–1813. New Delhi : O.U.P., 1988 : Appendices 1–3.
37. Chaudhuri, K.N. "Foreign Trade and Balance of Payments". Eds. Dharma Kumar and Meghnad Desai. *CEHI.* 2, New Delhi : Orient Longman, 1984 : 35.
38. Dutta, R.C. *Economic History of India Under the early British Rule,* Reprint, Publications Division, Ministry of Information and Broadcasting, New Delhi, 1973, pp. xxvi-xxvii. R.C. Dutt's figures, we should be careful to note, were not the assessed figures but the realized ones.
39. Firminger, W.K. *The Fifth Report from the Select Comitee of the House of Commons on the Affairs of the East India Company,* Augustus Kelly, New York, 1969, Ch. XVI : ccxviii-ccxix.
40. Furber, Holden. *John Company at Work....* 289.
41. De. The Cowrie Currency of India...., 10–11, H.R. Ghoshal, *Economic Transition in the Bengal Presidency.* Kolkata : Firma K.L. Mukhopadhyay, 1966 : 62, Amiya Kumar Bagchi: *Evolution of*

the State Bank...., 22.

42. Vogel. The Cowry Trade and the Economy of Yunnan...., 33–36.
43. Gupta, Ranjan. *Economic Life of a Bengal District....,* 238–41.
44. Mitra, K.P. "Currencies of Orissa". *Bengal Past and Present.* July-December, (1993) : 9–10.
45. Johnson. The Cowrie Currencies of West Africa...., Part II, 349–53.
46. Buchanan, Francis. *An Account of the Districts of Bihar and Patna in 1811–12,* Vol. II. *Bihar and Orissa Historical Research Society,* 1928 : 701.
    Buchanan, Francis. *An Account of the District of Sahabad, 1812–13. Bihar and Orissa Historical Research Society,* 1934 : 437–38.
47. Gupta, Ranjan. *Economic Life of a Bengal District....,* 242–43.
48. Mitra, Debendra Bijay. *Monetary System in the Bengal Presidency....* pp. 143–46, A. Siddiqi, "Money and Prices in the Early Stages of the Empire". *I.E.S.H.R.* 18, No. 3-4.
49. Bagchi. *Evolution of the State Bank....,* 108.
50. Buchanan, Frances. *An Account of the District of Purnea in 1809–10.* Bihar and Orissa Historical Research Society, 1928 : 586.
51. Yule and Burnell (eds): *Hobson-Jobson....,* 269.
52. Vogel. Cowry Trade and ...., 345–50.
53. Pressnell, L.S. *Country Banking in the Industrial Revolution.* Oxford: Clarendron Press, 1956 : 501–10.

Epilogue

In our discussion on two aspects of monetary transition in Bengal in the colonial period, we have seen that the transition was achieved through a protracted process unleashed by new forces and phenomena. It is also seen that the process did not represent a slow trend, but was ridden with conflicts and tensions. What was also evident was that economic phenomena like inflation were largely the product of the policies introduced by the new regime, such as expansion of monopoly trading and realization of exorbitant land revenue. Now a pertinent question may arise: can the subject of monetary transition, i.e. rise of some new forms of exchange, decline of old ones and establishment of some apparent order in place of the supposed earlier 'disorder' be studied in an isolated fashion? Or was it linked with other changes that were taking place in Bengal in the early colonial period, in the period of the Company rule? Or course, nobody would suggest that the transition in the monetary sphere was unrelated with these other changes, but the question is: what was the precise nature of this interrelation? Here we wish to argue that the process of transition should be conceived as a part of the overall structure of changes that the English Company was introducing in Bengal. Two important areas where these changes took place were the system of land entitlements and the control of market places. The former has been much discussed and debated, while the latter is rather neglected.

It is well known that the Permanent Settlement of land revenue was introduced in 1793. The significance of this

Settlement was that through it, the colonizing state assumed control over landed property in a predominantly agrarian economy. There is a widely held opinion that the Permanent Settlement created private property in land. In this opinion, it is ignored that the *zamindars* could retain their possession of this property only on condition of paying the revenue in proper time, and the Company assumed the right to realize the arrears, in case of default, by selling parts of the land possesed by the defaulting *zamindar* in auction. It is now a fact of history that many prominent *zamindars* lost their land in this process. In order to ensure the collection of revenue, the power of *zamindars* over *ryots* was enhanced by the Seventh Regulation of 1799.[1] This Regulation, commonly known as the *Haftam*, vested the *zamindars* with summary power to attach the defaulting ryots' property. Thus all the original pretensions declared at the time of the Settlement were thrown overboard. The majority of the old *zamindars* could not adust to this new situation and lost their property. Some big *zamindars* could retain their landholding through deceit and chicanery, which generally took the form of purchase through *benami* (puirchse of *mahals* in other names).[2] But they were too few in number. A few *zamindars* of lesser fame could adjust to the new situation, while many others perished.[3] The new *zamindars* that emerged in the process did not have the independence their predecessors had enjoyed in earlier times. As one of the most moted authorities on the operation of the Permanent Settlement has remarked, "The *zamindars*, as they stood preceding the British rule, arrogated to themselves immense privileges and power, thanks to decaying Mughal imperial power, and managed to occupy a significant place in the socio-political situation in the country...taking advantage of the fluidity of the politics of Subah-e-Bangla vis-a-vis the imperial politics the *zamindars* assumed immense legal and extra legal power upon themselves... The nawab tried to appease them by conferring on them the territorial titles of *rajas* and *maharajas* (kings, great kings). In addition to revenue collections they were given military and magisterial and judicial powers. In short, the great *zamindars* were state functionaries endowed with almost unlimited powers. Under the rules of the Permanent Settlement, these territorial potentates were shorn of all their powers and privileges. They were now reduced to ordinary individuals under district collectors."[4] It can only be said about the new *zamindars,* many of whom later received the titles of *Raja Bahadur* or *Maharaja* from their colonial masters, that they were more oppressive upon the *ryots* because otherwise they could not retain their status as *zamindars*. Their power over *ryots* has led some to believe that they were virtually independent sovereigns in their own domains. In reality, however, they were servile dependents.

The changed status of *zamindars* signified a fact; the colonizing state secured a position of complete hemenony over rural potentates. In this respect, just as in respect of the demonetization of the *cowrie,* the liberal British successfully achieved what the bureaucratic patrimonial Mughals had failed to attain.

It is perhaps not a coincidence that the introduction of the Permanent Settlement followed the introduction of the Company's copper coin, and that the time gap was not large. Both were symbols of the hegemony of the colonizing state. The year of the introduction of the copper pice, minted by an order from Warren Hastings, the then Governor General in Bengal, was possibly 1781-82. The process was taken up in earnest during 1790-93, when large amounts of copper coins, minted by Mathew Boulton began to be shipped to Bengal from Britain (we have already discussed this phenomenon). This temporal congruity cannot perhaps be brushed aside as merely coincidental. Just as the Permanent Settlement was an arm in the hands of the state to advance the process of colonization, so was the copper coin, which took the message of the new monetary order and of the Company's authority in this sphere to the countryside of Bengal. The twin process of advancement towards hegemony in the monetary sphere and subordinating the rural potentates ran concurrently. One can link it with the introduction of Cornwallis's monetary reform of 1792, prohibiting the use of all other rupee currencies except the 19th Sun *sicca*.

Trying to minimize the role of the colonizing state in the far-reaching changes and to uphold the thesis of some sort of 'continuity' might lead to gross mistakes in generalization.

One example may be given to illustrate the point. C.A. Bayly has commented on the landholding class of the 19th century, "....many of the features of the nineteenth century landed class were consolidated in the eighteenth century. The weakening of the Mughal power enabled local gentry to seize privileges, which they had once been denied. Zamindars (landholders) began to tax markets and to seize prebendal lands which the Mughal elites had once tried to keep out of their hands."[5] while the second part of this paragraph (The weakening... their hands) contains a large measure of truth—although the Mughals could not attain complete success in denying those privileges—those privileges were not features of the new landholding class that emerged in the 19th century in the wake of the Permanent Settlement. Bayly's scholarship is not quite impeccable in this respect. It is clear that the noted social historian has not tried to findout whether the advent of the Company as the ruler did not introduce any qualitative change or break in the sociao-economic scenario. He has also failed to understand that the new landlords were by and large creatures of the British.

Another point, also related with the colonization process and the monetary transition, was that of the changes taking place in respect of the institution of market. The markets had earlier been controlled by *zamindars*, nawabs and kings and were often linked with religious and charitable institutions. There were some markets that were *lakheraj* or rent-free. About the year 1790 there reportedly existed in the district of Murshidabad 28 *lakheraj gainjs* or regular markets (some *ganjs* in all probability escaped the notice of the authorities).[6] Such *ganjs* and *haats* generally served as income-earning establishments for persons of noble birth and charitable and religious institutions. There were, however, markets whose income was more widely distributed. "A *haat* established in Khurrapur, *pargana* Satsika (near Halsihahar), by Habibullah Chaudhuri under the *sanad* (written authority) of the *Zamindar* in 1750, was paying revenue to local rulers as well as to the temple of the local deity."[7] Besides, there were various *zamindari ghats*, i.e. river points from which tolls were collected. And duties were also traditionally collected for protection or roads (*rahadari*).

The Company issued an order in 1772 abolishing all toll stations. It has been interpreted as a policy to liberate trade. But actually, this order was followed, after a certain time lag, by the assumption by the Company of the sole right to impose custom duties at standardized rates.[8] In 1793, the same year when the Permanent Settlement of land revenue was introduced, all *lakheraj ganjs* and the right of native *zamindars* to collect market dues were abolished.[9] This measure was sought to be justified by the argument that it would liberate trade from the interference and oppression by native potentates. There are at least some historians who have tried to assert that the measures of the Company liberated trade from the constraints influenced by earlier rulers. For example, K.M. Mohsin, referring to the order of 1793, has commented, "It was only when Cornwallis abolished all *lakheraj ganjs* and collection of market dues in 1793 that the process of legislating for complete freedom of internal trade was completed."[10] It is interesting that anohter noted scholar, while writing about the status of traders in Mughal India, has commented, "It was not until the English East India Company began to extend its control over the subcontinent in the late eighteenth and early nineteenth centuries and introduced the principles of private property, sanctity of contract, and rule of law that a true market economy hospitable to merchants began to develop."[11] What is implied in this view is that markets in earlier regimes were severely constrained and had an essentially local character. In our discussion of the economy of pre-colonial Bengal in general, we have pointed out that Bengal used to supply rice, butter, sugar, etc. to far-flung areas, besides cotton textiles and raw silk. Bengal also used to import cotton on a large scale. Whatever the constraints imposed by provincial rulers and local potentates, they could not destroy or even curb this long-distance trade through which Bengal had been integrated into a market of subcontinental dimension and acquired an important place for herself in the commercial map of India. It is true that this process of market formation was very much incomplete but one cannot deny that this process was in existence. Besides, it should be taken into account that the English East India Company was by itself a commercial power, combining its target of revenue collection with that of profit maximization from trade. So, the policy of abolishing *zamindari* and other restrictions with the declared aim of liberating trade was fraught with contradictions arising out of the nature of the motivations of the Company itself. Trade in grains was to some extent freed, and grain merchants possibly got some more space compared with earlier times. Merchants set up markets at their own initiative in some regions and hence the number of markets grew.[12] It is also quite possible that some sort of synchronization in respect of grain prices was established.[13] We cannot however ascertain to what extent it was a general phenomenon because the evidence is scanty. But the Company's monopolization of the trade of some important commodities like salt, opium, raw silk and cotton is an incontrovertible historical fact. This monopolization created a formidable barrier to the implementation of the doctrine of free trade. So, it remains a moot question as to how far the measures for controlling the market places liberated commerce, and along with it, the indigenous traders of Bengal as a whole. After all, the Company was itself a commercial power, and could not afford to be too much interested in the prosperity of indigenous traders. So, there is a great deal of justification in the thesis put forward by one scholar, that "sequestration of market places from its traditional lineage, the rapid expansion of police and custom outposts in order to govern them, and, finally, the relentless effort to standardize money, bills, and currency were the inexorable consequences of the process of colonization."[14]

Distinguished historians have described in detail the activities of the Company as a commercial power with monopolistic designs. It should be noted that this monopolization radically changed the position of indigenous intermediaries. Here we wish to illustrate the point with a particular example, namely the transformation of the role of the *pykars* (cocoon traders) in the silk industry under colonial rule. Gautam Bhadra has meticulously studied the interactions among various classes *gomastas, pykars* and *chassars* (primary producers) involved in the production and intermediate marketing of silk during the period 1765-1830. The relation between the *pykars* and the Company went through a number of stages. The *pykars,* in the earlier part of the period the study is concerned with, gained greater wealth by increasing their hold over primary producers as well as by acting as short-term financiers of the Company and also by virtue of having a better bargaining power than other middlemen. Many of them set up their own filiatures (cocoon-rearing units) also. But the repressive arm of the Company began to show itself in course of time. The Company, in order to control the production process, began to hire these filiatures and often compelled the *pykars* to rent them by use of force.[15] The concluding remark of Bhadra is worth quoting.

"With the destruction of filiatures and with de-industrialization, the *pykars* (at least those owing filiatures) had no scope of developing into manufacturers. They were integrated into the Company's trading system through advances and through administrative pressure and assistance. It no doubt gave them more power over the *chassars,* helped them to acquire more wealth than their predecessors in precolonial Bengal. On the other hand, it did not chart out any independent course of development for them. The whole process reveals that divorce from land and development into a fully commercial class was not their fate because that would not help in supplying only raw material to the Company."[16] Monopolization on such a scale was unknown to the pre-colonial market; rather, it was very much like the state stepping to constrain it, and acting as an obstacle to its freedom. Just as the Permanent Settlement was a caricature of the English system of landed property, as Marx put it,[17] the so-called market reform was a caricature of the British view of laissez faire.

What we wish to point out is that the notion of so-called liberation of trade in the colonial period is largely illusory, based on the ole belief in the civilizing mission of British rule in India. The liberation of grain trade, although couched in terms of the language of 'free trade', was necessary for the Company for having an ample supply for the new urban centers, mainly Calcutta (Kolkata), which grew up under the umbrella of the Company. It may be added that trade in food grains was immeasurably trickier to handle than that in salt, opium and raw silk, because unlike the latter, the production of rice was an activity common to the whole of rural Bengal.

In short, it can be argued that the market, as it evolved in the colonial period, was within a twilight zone, free in some respects but strangulated in others. While some of the extra-economic power of landed potentates was taken away, and some degree of uniformity of rule was achieved, the basis of feudal exploitation through surplus appropriation by extra-economic means was retained, and the new *zamindars,* mostly absentee landlords, were no less oppressive than the old ones. In a similar fashion, some degree of market integration was achieved, but state control was imposed in a new guise, as a process of creating a colonial terrain. One can find something like simultaneous destruction and preservation of the old order of things in the contradictory nature of the changes that engulfed Bengal in the process of colonization.

It should be made clear that during the process of monetary transition, many interests were involved. The formation of so-called 'modern' institutions of banking was also a field where different interests clashed. The Bank of Bengal was set up in December 1808. It was virtually the bank of the Government. But in 1819, the Commercial Bank was opened, and in 1824, the Calcutta Bank was founded. In 1829, the Union Bank was started by the partners of the Commercial Bank. This joint-stock bank represented private interests and became the chief competitor of the Bank of Bengal. Unable to withstand the commercial crisis of 1846-47, this bank collapsed in the late 1840s and was finally liquidated in 1850. Prince Dwaraka Nath Tagore, the grandfather of Rabindranath Tagore, was closely associated with the Union Bank till his death (1 August 1945) and according to the historian of his commercial and industrial activities, one of the factors leading to the fall of the Union Bank was the "hands-off policy of the Government."[18] Government patronage was not, however, denied to the Bank of Bengal.[19] In other words, Adam Smith's invisible hand was only too visible in this matter also. We may call it a caricature of the English classical political economy as well.

One more point may be brought in for preliminary discussion. The process of colonization was finally completed with the transfer of power from the Company to the Crown, when the Industrial Revolution in Britain has reached its triumphant conclusion and India had been transformed, with the help of railways and steamships, into the servitor economy of British industrial capital. It is interesting that in this process, the powers of the English East India Company, which started the colonization of India, were gradually curbed. The monetary measures initiated under the Company were inherited by Her Majesty's Government of India. One section of the people, apparently overwhelmed by the new objects and institutions, regarded them as the manifestations of a new and just order. The attitude of the luminaries of the 'Bengal Renaissance', whose outlook was definitely warped by the combination of the creation of the 'landlord's paradise and the dazzles of the new ideas brought to them by the contacts with the West, to the order brought into being by the colonzing state is well known. But less known is the fact that the faith in *Pax Britannica* penetrated the minds of the less enlightened as well.

We here provide an example. It is a poem, written by one Munshi Alimuddin. In its English rendering (it is interesting that the poet belonged to the Muslim literati, which in general had boycotted English education during the period of Company rule), the poem is:

The people are governed with full justice
In her reign, the praja have no complaints,
Cowries have been abolished; now
People buy what they need with coins
People exchange news through mail.
The towns are now lit with gaslights.
The stamer has vanquished the pinnace and the sailboat,
The railway has reduced a week's journey to hours.
In Calcutta they can find out what's happening in England

In a matter of moments—with the help of the wire.[20]

Interestingly enough, the writer has conceived the monetary changes like the replacement of the *cowrie* by the government-sponsored metallic coin as a phenomenon that is linked with changes in the spheres of transport and communications as part of an integrated whole, as part of a new order. The writer was perceptive enough, but pitifully unmindful of the process though which this transformation had been achieved, and the costs that had to be paid and the identity of the payers. These payers of course refused to submit and they frequently rose in revolt. The history of peasant revolts in colonial India is as colourful as the history of the changes brought about by the colonizing state and the collaborating modernizers, but that is another story.

The illusion finally broke in the 20th century and the literati began to challenge the legitimacy of colonial rule.

NOTES AND REFERENCES

1. Islam, Sirajul. *The Permanent Settlement—A Study of its Operation* 1790–1819. Dacca : Bangla Academy, 1979 : 65–75.
2. One notable example is that of the Raja of Burdwan, vide Harashankar Bhattacharya: *Zamindars and Patnidars,* University of Burdwan, 1984, Ch. II, 40–72 Passim. For a brief account of the method of working of such transactions, Islam: Ibid, 151–54.
3. One example of the survival of smaller, but yet wealthy *zamindars* is that of Bhawal, Dacca. For a brief history of the estate of Bhawal, Patha Chatterjee: *A Princely Impostor?—The Kumar of Bhawal and the Secret History of Indian Nationalism.* Delhi : Permanent Black, 2004 : 15–25 Chatterjee has not discussed how the Bhawal estate could escape the fate that befell many *zamindars,* presumably for the reason that the main theme of his book is a sensational story around a son of the *zamindar* family, who supposedly returned as a monk more than ten years after his assumed death and cremation.
4. Islam, Sirajul. "The Permanent Settlement and the Peasant". In *History of Bangladesh,* Vol. 2. Ed. Idem. *Asiatic Society of Bangladesh,* 1992 : 251–53.
5. Bayly, C.A. *Indian Society and the Making of the British Empire,*

New Cambridge History of India, II. I. C.U.P., Orient Longman, 1988 : 9–10.

6. Mohsin, K.M. *A Bengal District in Transition: Murshidabad* 1765–1793. Dacca : Bangla Academy, 1973 : 100–102.
7. Sen, Sudipta. *The Empire of Free Trade.* Philadelphia : Pensylvania University Press, 1999 : 53.
8. For a fairly detailed account, Sen: Ibid, Ch. 5, 144–165, passim.
9. Mohsin: Ibid; pp. 103–104. Sen: Ibid: p. 140.
10. Mohsin: Ibid, p. 110.
11. Blake, Stephen. *Shahjahanabad.* C.U.P., 1993 : 112.
12. Datta, Rajat. *Society, Economy and the Market, Commercialization in Rural Bengal*, c1760–1800. New Delhi : Manohar, 2000 : 205–06.
13. Ibid, pp. 197–200.
14. Sen, Sudipta. *The Empire of Free Trade*, 17.
15. Bhadra, Gautam, The Role of *Pykars* in the Silk Industry of Bengal c1765–1830. *Studies in History*, 1987.
16. Ibid, 35.
17. Marx, Karl. *Dascapital.* Vol. III. Moscow: 1986 : Ch. XX, ftn. 50.
18. On the history of the Union Bank, Blair B. Kling: *Parnter in Empire: Dearakanath Tagore and the Age of Enterprise in Eastern India.* Kolkata: Firma K.L. Mukhopadhyay, 1981 : 42–43 and Ch. IX, 230–246, passim.
19. Bagchi, Amiya Kumar. *Evolution of the State Bank of India*, Vol. I., Part I, 169.
20. Quoted in Partha Chatterjee: *The Nation and its Fragments—Colonian and Post Colonial Histories.* O.U.P., 1994 : 86–87.

Select Bibliography

PRINTED PRIMARY SOURCES

1. Buchanan, Francis. *An Account of the District of Purnea, 1809.*
2. Bihar and Orissa Historical Research Society, 1928
3. ______ . *An Account of the District of Sahabad 1813–14,* Bihar and Orissa Historical Research Society, 1934, Delhi edition 1986.
4. ______ . *An Account of the Districts of Patna and Bihar, 1811–12,* Bihar and Orissa Historical Research Society, 1928.
5. Chakrabarty, Mukundaram. *Chandimangal.* Ed. Sukumar Sen: Sahitya Akedemi, 1993.
6. Phillips, C.H. (ed): *The Correspondences of Lord William Cavendish Bentinck,* 1828–31. O.U.P., 1977.
7. Firminger, W.T. *The Fifth Report From the Select Committee of the House of Commons on the Affairs of the East India Company.* Reprint. New York: Augustus Kelly, 1969.
8. N.K. Sinha et al. (eds). *Fort William–India House Correspondences,* Delhi: National Archives of India.
9. Hunter, W.W. *Annals of Rural Bengal.* Reprint. Kolkata: Government of West Bengal, 1997.
10. Marriot, John and Mukhopadhyay, Bhaskar (eds.) : *Britain in India* 1765–1905. London: Pickering & Chatto, 2006.
11. Tavernier, J.B. *Travels in India.* Trl. V. Ball : Reprint. Delhi : Munshiram Manoharlal, 1995.
12. Wilson, C.R. *The Early Annals of the English in Bengal.* Reprint. Kolkata : Asiatic Society of Bengal, 1996.

Articles

1. "Ahmed, Sharifuddin. Urbanization and Urban Classes". In Sirajul Islam (ed): *History of Bangladesh,* Vol. 1. Dhaka: Asiatic Society of Bangladesh, 1992 : 203–238.

2. Arasaratnam, S. "India and the Indian Ocean in the Seventeenth Century". In *India and the Indian Ocean* 1500–1800. Eds. Ashin Das Gupta and M.N. Pearson, O.U.P., 1999.
3. Ceylon in the Indian Ocean Trade 1500–1800, in the same volume.
4. _____. The Rice Trade in Eastern India, 1650–1740. *M.A.S.* 22, no. 3 (1988).
5. Atwell, William S. "International Bullion Flows and the Chinese Economy circa 1530–1650". *Past and Present.* (February 1982).
6. Awwal, Iftikar-ul. "The State of Indigenous Industries". In *History of Bangladesh,* Vol. II. Ed. Sirajul Islam. Dhaka: Asiatic Society of Bangladesh, 1992.
7. Bagchi, A.K. "Transition from Indian to British–Indian Money and Banking." *M.A.S.* 19, no. 3 (1995).
8. _____. Money and Credit as Areas of Conflict, Mimeographed, *Centre for Studies in Social Sciences,* 1982.
9. Banerjee, Kumkum. "Grain Traders and the East India Company: Patna and its Hinterland." In *Merchants, Markets and the State in Early Modern India.* Ed. Subrahmanyam. India: O.U.P., 1990.
10. Bhadra, Gautam. "The Role of Pykars in the Silk Industry of Bengal, (c1765–1830)". *Studies in History,* 1987.
11. Blake, Stephen. "The Structure of Monetary Exchange in North India." In *The Imperial Monetary System of Mughal India.* Ed. J.F. Richards. India: O.U.P., 1987.
12. Braudel and Spooner. "Price in Europe from 1450 to 1750". *Cambridge Economic History of Europe,* Vol. IV. Ed. Rich and Wilson. Cambridge: 1967.
13. Brenner, Robert. "Agrarian Class Structure and Economic Development in Pre-Industrial Europe". In *The Brenner Debate.* Eds. T.H. Ashton and C.H.E. Phillipin. C.U.P., South Asian Edition, 2005.
14. _____. Agrarian Roots of European Capitalism, in the same volume.
15. Brennig, Joseph. "Chief Merchants and the European Enclaves of Seventeenth Century Coromande." *M.A.S.* 11, no. 3 (1977).
16. _____. Textile Production and Producers in Late Seventeenth Century Coromandel. In *Merchants, Markets and the State in Early Modern India.* Ed. Sanjay Subrahmanyam. O.U.P., 1990.
17. Broadberry, Stephen and Gupta. Bishnupriya. "The Early Modern Great Divergence, Wages, Prices and Economic Development in Europe and Asia, *Economic History Review,* LIX

(I) (February 2006).

18. Chakrabarty, Subhra. "Intransigent Shroffs and the English East India Company's Currency Reforms in Bengal, 1757–1800". *I.E.S.H.R.* 34, no. 1 (1997).
19. ______ . Major Shifts in India's Trade and Commercial Organizations, 1700–1860. In *Economic History of India from the Eighteenth to the Twentieth Century*. Ed. Binay Bhusan Chudhuri. Delhi: Centre for Studies in Civilizations, 2005.
20. Chandra, Satish. "Commercial Activities of the Mughal Emperors during the Seventeenth Century." In *Essays in Mediaeval Indian Economic History*. Ed. Idem. Delhi : Munshiram Manoharlal, 1987.
21. Chatterjee, Kumkum. "Collaboration and Conflict; Bankers and the Early Colonial Rule in India, 1757–1813". *I.E.S.H.R* 30, no. 3 (1993).
22. Chauduri, K.N. "Towards an Intercontinental Model : Some Trends in Indo-European Trade in the Seventeenth Century". *I.E.S.H.R* 6, no. 1 (1969).
23. ______ . "Foreign Trade and Balance of Payments." *C.E.H.I.* II, Orient Longman, 1984.
24. ______ . Markets and Traders in India in the Seventeenth and Eighteenth Centuries. In *Money and Market in India*, 1100–1700. Ed. Sanjay Subrahmanyam. O.U.P. 1994.
25. Chaudhuri, Sushil. "The Financing of Investments in Bengal 1650–1720". *I.E.S.H.R.* 8, no. 2 (1971).
26. ______ . "Merchants, Companies and Rulers". *J.E.S.H.O.* 31, no. 1 (1988).
27. ______ . "General Economic Conditions Under the Nawabs". In *History of Bangladesh*, Vol. II. Ed. Sirajul Islam. Dhaka: Asiatic Society of Bangladesh, 1992.
28. ______ . European Companies and the Export Trade in the Eighteenth Century, in the same volume, pp. 183–224.
29. Dasgupta, Ashin. "The Merchants of Surat, c1700–1750". In *Elites of South Asia*. Ed. Leach and Mukherjee. C.U.P., 1970.
30. ______ . "Trade and Politics in Eighteenth Century India. In *The Mughal State*, 1500–1800. Ed. Alam and Subrahmanyam. O.U.P., 1997.
31. ______ . "Indian Merchants and Trade in the Indian Ocean c.1500–1700" Ed. Habib and Raychaudhuri *C.E.H.I.* Vol 1, Orient Longman, 1982.
32. ______ . "Indian Merchants and the Western Indian Oceans". *M.A.S.* 19, no. 3 (1985).

33. Datta, Rajat. "Merchants and Peasants: A Study of the Structure of Local Trade in Late Eighteenth century Bengal". In *Merchants, Markets and the State....*, Ed. Sanjay Subrahmanyam.
34. Dey, Sushil Chandra. "The Cowrie Currency of India". *Orissa Historical Journal*, 1, no. 1 (1952).
35. Deyell, John. S. "The Development of Akbar's Currency System and Monetary Integration of the Conquered Kingdoms". In *The Imperial Monetary System of Mughal India.* Ed. J.F. Richards.
36. Dobb, Maurice. Reply to Paul Sweezy, Ed. Rodney Hilton: *The Transition from Feudalism to Capitalism.* Delhi: Aakar Books, 2006.
37. Fukazawa, H. "The State and the Economy, Maharastra and the Deccan: A Note". *C.E.H.I.* 1.
38. Glamann, K. European Trade, 1500–1700, C.M. Cipolla (ed): *The Fontana Economic History of Europe: The Sixteenth and Seventeenth Centuries.* Glasgow: Collins/Fontana, 1974.
39. Gordon, Stewart. "The Slow Conquest, Administrative Integration of Malwa into the Maratha Empire, 1720–1760". *M.A.S.* 12, no. 1 (1977).
40. _____. "Burhanpur; Entrepot and Hinterland 1650–1750". *I.E.S.H.R.* 25, no. 4 (1988).
41. Habib, Irfan: "The System of Bills of Exchange in Mughal India". In *Essays in Medieval Indian Economic History.* Ed. Satish Chandra. Delhi : Munshiram Manoharlal, 1987.
42. "Potentialities of Capitalist Development in Mughal India". *Journal of Economic History.* (December 1969). Reprinted in *Essays in Indian History.* Idem. Delhi: Tulika, 1995.
43. _____. "Agrarian Relations and Land Revenue". Eds. Habib and Raychaudhuri. *C.E.H.I.*, I.
44. _____. "Monetary System of Trimetallism in the Age of the Price Revolution". In *The Imperial Monetary System of Mughal India.* Ed. J.F. Richards.
45. Haider, Najaf. "Precious Metal Flows and Currency Circulation in the Mughal Empire". *J.E.S.H.O.* 39, no. 3 (1996).
46. _____. "The Monetary Basis of Credit and Banking Instruments in the Mughal Empire". In *Money and Credit in Indian History.* Ed. Amiya Bagchi. Delhi: Tulika, 2002.
47. Hambly, Gavin. "Towns and Cities". *CEHI*, I.
48. Hasan, Aziza. "The Silver Currency Output of the Mughal Empire and Prices in India in the Sixteenth and Seventeenth Centuries". *I.E.S.H.R.* 6, no. 2 (1969).
49. _____. "Mints of the Mughal Empire". In *Essays in Medieval Indian Economic History.* Ed. Satish Chandra.

50. Islam, Sirajul. "Permanent Settlement and the Peasant". In *History of the Bangladesh,* Vol. II. Ed. Idem.
51. Johnson, Marion. "The Cowrie Currencies of West Africa". *Journal of African History.* XI (1 & 3), 1970.
52. Karim, Abdul. "Mughal Revenue System". In *History of Bangladesh,* Vol. I. Ed. Sirajul Islam.
53. Kulkarni, G.T. "Banking in the Eighteenth century: A Case Study of a Poona Banker". *Artha Vijnana*: XV (June 1973).
54. Kulkarni, A.R. "Money and Banking Under the Marathas : Seventeenth Century to AD 1848". *Money and Credity in Indian History.* Ed. Amiya Bagchi.
55. Leonard, Karen. "The Great Firm Theory of the Decline of the Mughal Empire". *C.S.S.H.* 21, no. 1 (1979), reprinted in *The Mughal State.* Ed. Alam and Subrahmanyam.
56. Mohsin, K.M. "Banking in Mughal Bengal. *History of Bangladesh,* Vol. II. Ed. Sirajul Islam. Dhaka: Asiatic Society of Bangladesh, 1992.
57. Moosvi, Shireen. "The Silver Influx, Money Supply, Prices and Revenue Extraction in Mughal India". *J.E.S.H.O.* 30, no. 1 (1987).
58. ______. "Gujarati Ports and their Hinterlands". In *Ports and their Hinterlands in India.* Ed. Indu Banga. Delhi : Manohar, 1992.
59. ______. "A Note on the Interest Rates in the Seventeenth the early Eighteenth Centuries. *Money and Credit.....* Ed. Bagchi.
60. ______. "The Indian Economic Experience 1600–1900: A Quantitative Study" In *The Making of Indian History, Essays Presented to Irfan Habib.* Eds. K.N. Panikkar, Terence J. Byres and Utsa Pattanaik. Delhi: Tulika, 200.
61. Neale, Walter. "Reciprocity and Redistribution in the Indian Village: Sequel to some Noble Discussions". In *Markets and Trade in Early Empires.* Eds. Polanyi, Arsenbrg and Pearson. The Free Press Illinois and the Falcon's Wing Press, 1957.
62. Newitt, M.D.D. "East Africa and Indian Ocean Trade 1500-1800". Eds. In *India and the Indian Ocean....* Dasgupta and Pearson.
63. Parker, Geoffrey. "The Emergence of Modern Finance in Europe, 1500–1730". In *The Fontana Economic History of Europe: The Sixteenth and Seventeenth Centuries.* Ed. Carl. M. Cipolla.
64. Perlin, Frank. "Mint Technology and Mint Output in an Age of Growing Commercialization". In *Essays in Medieval Indian Economic History.* Ed. Satish Chandra : Money Use in Late Precolonial India and International Trade in Currency media. In *The Imperial Monetary System of Mughal India.* Ed. J.F. Richards.
65. ______. "Changes in Production and Circulation of Money in

Seventeenth and Eighteenth Century India : An Essay in Circulation and Decline, In *Money and Market in India....* Ed. Subrahmanyam.

66. _____. "Commercial Manufacture and the Proto-Industrialization Thesis." In *Unbroken Landscape,* Varorium, Ashgate and Hampshire, 1994. Ed. Idem.
67. _____ . "Monetary Revolution and Societal Change in Late Medieval and Early Modern Times". In *The Invisible City*. Idem. Ashgate and Hampshire: Varorium, 1994.
68. Polanyi, Karl. "The Economy as Instituted Process". In *Market and Trade in the Early Empires.* Eds. Polanyi, Arsenberg and Pearson.
69. Prakash, Om. "Bullion for Goods; International Trade and the Economy of Early Eighteenth Century Bengal. *I.E.S.H.R.* XIII, (2), 1976. "The Indian Maritime Merchant", 1500–1800. *J.E.S.H.O.* 47, no. 3 (2004).
70. _____."On Coinage in Mughal India". *I.E.S.H.R.*, XXV (4) : 1988.
71. _____. "Foreign Merchants and Indian Mints in the Seventeenth and the Early Eighteenth Century". In *The Imperial Monetary System of Mughal India*. Ed. Richards.
72. _____ . "The System of Credit in Mughal India". In *Money and Credit.....* Ed. Amiya Bagchi.
73. Ray, Indrani. "Indian in Asian Trade in the 1730s; A Discussion by a French Trader". Ed. Barun De. In *Essays Presented to Prof. S.C. Sarkar*. Delhi : People's Publishing House, 1976.
74. Raychaudhuri Tapan. "The Agrarian System of Mughal India: A Review Essay, Enquiry, 1965". Reprinted in *The Mughal State.* Eds. Alam and Subrahmanyam.
75. _____ . "The State and the Economy". *C.E.H.I.* I.
76. _____. "Non-agricultural Production". In the same volume.
77. _____. "Inland Trade" In the same volume.
78. Richards, J.F. "Official Revenue and Money Flows in a Mughal Province". In *The Imperial Monetary System.....*Ed. Idem.
79. _____ . "Mughal State Finance and the Pre-modern World Economy". *C.S.S.H.* 23, no. 3 (1981).
80. Sarkar, Smritikumar. "Social Organization of Artisan Production in India: Changing Role of Market, Technology and Merchant Creditor: the 18th to the 20th Centuries. In *Economic History of India from the Eighteenth to the Twentieth Century*. Ed. Binay Chadhuri.
81. Sharma, Ramesh Chandra. "Aspects of Business of Northern India in the Seventeenth Century. In *Essays in Medieval Indian*

Economic History. Ed. Satish Chandra.

82. Sinha, N.K. "Introduction to Salt Papers". *The Historian as Archivist* (Selected Papers of N.K. Sinha), Kolkata: 1997.
83. Subrahmanyan, Lazmi. "Banias and the British; The Role of Indigenous Credit in the Process of Imperial, Expansion in Western India in the Second half of the Eighteenth Century. *M.A.S.* 21, no. 3 (1987).
84. Subrahmanyam, Sanjay. "The Portuguese, the Port of Basrur and the Rice Trade, 1600–1650". In *Merchants, Markets and the State*.....Ed. Idem.
85. _____ . "Rural Industry and Commercial Agriculture in late Seventeenth Century South Eastern India". *Past and Present* (February, 1990).
86. _____ . "The Mughal State, Structure or Process? Reflections on Recent Western Historiography." *I.E.S.H.R.* 29, No. 3 (1992).
87. _____ . "Precious Metal Flows and Prices in Wetern and Southern Asia—Some Conjunctural Variations". In *Money and Market*..... Ed. Idem.
88. Sweezy, Paul. "A Critique of Maurice Dobb's 'Studies in the Development of Capitalism". In *The Transition from Feudalsim to Capitalism*. Ed. Rodney Hilton.
89. Vogel, Hans-Ulrich. "Cowry Trade and its Role in the Economy of Yunnan". *J.E.S.H.O.* 36, no. 2&3 (1993).
90. Surndorfer Harriet T. "Another look at China—Money, Silver and the Seventeenth Century Crisis". *J.E.S.H.O* 42, no. 3 (1999).

Books

1. Anderson, Perry. *The Lineages of the Absolutist State*, N.L.B, 1974.
2. Arasaratnam, S. *Merchants, Companies and Commerce on the Coromandel Coast*, O.U.P. 1996.
3. _____ . *Maritime Trade in India in the Seventeenth Century*, O.U.P. 1997.
4. Athar Ali, M. *Aurangseber Amale Mughal Abhijat Sreni* (The Mughal Nobility under Aurangzeb) Translated by Arun Kumar De, K.P. Bagchi, Kolkat, 1978.
5. Bagchi, Amiya Kumar. *The Political Economy of Underdevelopment*, Indian edition, Orient Longman, 1989.
6. _____ . *The Evolution of the State Bank of India*, Voll I, Part I, O.U.P. 1986.
7. Bayly, C.A. *Rulers, Townsmen and Bazars, North Indian Society in the Age of British Expansion*, 1770–1879 C.U.P. 1983.
8. _____ . *Indian Society and the Making of the British Empire, New*

Cambridge History of India 2.1, Orient Longman, 1988.
9. Bhadra, Gautam: *Mughal Juge Krishi Arthaniti O Krishak Bidroha* (The Agrarian Economy and Peasant Rebellions in the Mughal Era) in Bengali, Subarnarekha, Kolkata, 1991.
10. Bhaduri, Amit. *Macroeconomics; The Dynamics of Commodity Production,* Macmillan 1986.
11. Bhattacharya, Harashankar. *Zamindars and Patnidars,* The University of Burdwan, 1985.
12. Bhattacharya, Sukumari. *In Those Days, Essays Vedic—Epic and Classical,* Kolkata: Camp., 2001.
13. Blake, Stephen. *Shahjahanabad,* C.U.P. Indian Edition, 1993. Braudel, F : *Capitalism in Material Life 1400*–1800. Glasgow: Collins/Fontana, 1974.
14. Chandra, Satish. *Mogal Darbare Dal O Rajniti* 1707–1740, (Parties and Politics at the Mughal Court). Trl by Chandika Prasad Bandopadhyay. Kolkata: K.P. Bagchci, 1978.
15. Chatterjee, Partha. *The Nation and its Fragments.* O.U.P., 1994.
16. ______ . *A Princely Impostor?—The Kumar of Bhawal and the Secret History of Indian Nationalism.* Delhi: Permanent Black, 2004.
17. Chattopadhyay, B.D. *The Making of Early Medieval India.* O.U.P., 1994.
18. Chaudhuri, K.N. *The Trading World of Asia and the English East India Company 1660*–1760. C.U.P., 1978.
19. Chaudhuri, Sushil. *Trade and Commercial Organization in Bengal 1640*–1720. Kolkata: Firma K.L. Mukhopadhyay, 1976.
20. ______ . *From Prosperity to Decline—Bengal in the Eighteenth Century,* Delhi : Manohar, 1995.
21. Chown, John. *A History of Money, From A.D. 800.* London and New York: Routledge, 1996.
22. Dasgupta, Ashin. *Indian Merchants and the Decline of Surat 1700*–1750. Wiesbaden: 1979.
23. ______ . *Bangopasagar* (The Bay of Bengal) in Bengali. Kolkata L Pratikshan Publications, 1989.
24. Datta, Rajat. *Society Economy and the Market—Commercialization in Rural Bengal c1760*–1800. Delhi : Manohar, 2000.
25. Deyell, John S. *Living without Silver,* Reprint, O.U.P., 1999.
26. Feldback, Ole, *India Trade under the Danish Flag* 1772–1808. Student Literature, 1969.
27. Fischer, David Hackett. *The Great Wave—Price Revolutions and the Rhythm of History.* New York: O.U.P., 2004.
28. Furber, Hoden. *John Company at Work—A Study of European Expansion in the Late Eighteenth Century.* Cambridge: Harvard

University Press, 1948.

29. Ghosal, H.R. *Economic Transition in the Bengal Presidency.* Kolkata: Firma K.L. Mukhopadhyay, 1966.
30. Ghosal, Sarat Chandra. *A History of Coochbiher.* Reprint. Siliguri: N.L. Publishers, 2005.
31. Gupta, Ranjan. *The Economic Life of a Bengal District,* Birbhun 1770–1857 Burdwan: University of Burdwan, 1984.
32. ______. *Rahrer Samaj, Arthaniti O Gana Bidroha,* (in Bengali). Calcutta : Subarnarekha, 2001.
33. Habib, Irfan. *The Agrarian System of Mughal India.* Bombay: Asia Publishing House, 1963.
34. ______. *An Atlas of the Mughal Empire.* O.U.P., 1986.
35. Hamilton, Earl J. *American Trasure and the Price Revilution in Spain,* 1501–1650. Massachusets: Cambridge, 1936.
36. Hicks, J.R. *Theory of Economic History.* Oxford : Clarendon Press, 1969.
37. Hogendron, Jan and Johnson, Marion: *Shell Money and Slave Trade.* C.U.P., 1986.
38. Hussain, Hameeda. *The Company Weavers of Bengal: The East India company and the Organization of Textile Production in Bengal,* 1750–1813. O.U.P., 1988.
39. Hussain, Syed Izaz. *The Bengal Sultanate; Politics, Economy and Coins,* (AD 1205–1576). Delhi : Manohar, 2003.
40. Islam, Sirajul. *The Permanent Settlement in Bengal—A Study of its Operations,* 1790–1819. Dhaka : Bangla Academy, 1979.
41. Keynes, J.M. *A Treatise on Money.* London : Macmillan, 1930.
42. Kling, Blair B. *Partner in Empire; Dwarakanath Tagore and the Age of Enterprise in Eastern India,* Kolkata: Firma K.L.M., 1981.
43. Majumdar, Arun. *Structural Evolution of the Indian Economy, Early Phase.* Delhi : Manohar, 1992.
44. Malcom, John. *A Memoir of Central India,* Vol. II. Delhi: Sagar Publications, 1970.
45. Marshall, Peter. *East Indian Fortunes—The British in Bengal in the Eighteenth Century.* Oxford : Oxford University Press, 1976.
46. Marx, Karl. *Dascapital,* Vol. I & III. Moscow: 1986.
47. Misra, K.P. *Benaras in Transition.* Delhi : Manohar, 1975.
48. Mitra, Debendra Bijay. *Monetary System in the Bengal Presidency 1757–1835,* Kolkata: K.P. Bagchi, 1991.
49. Mohsin, K.M. *A Bengal District in Transition, Murshidabad 1765–1793.* Dhaka : Bangla Academy, 1973.
50. Moosvi, Shireen, *The Economy of the Mughal Empire* c1595—A Statistical Study, O.U.P., 1986.

51. Moreland. *The Agrarian System of Moslem India.* Reprint. Delhi : Oriental Books Reprints Corporation, 1968.
52. ______ . From *Akbar to Aurangzeb.* Reprint. Delhi : Munshilal Manoharlal, 1990.
53. Naqvi, H.K., *Urban Centres and Industries in Upper India* 1536–1803. Bombay : Asia Publishing House, 1968.
54. ______ . *Urbanisation and Urban Centres Under the Great Mughals* 1556–1707. Simla: Institute of Advanced Studies, 1971.
55. Prakash, Om. *The Dutch East India Company and the Economy of Bengal,* 1640–1730. O.U.P., 1988.
56. Pressnol, L.S. *Country Banking in the Industrial Revolution,* Oxford: Clarendron Press, 1956.
57. Ray, Nihar Ranjan. *Bangalir Itihas, Adi Parba* (A History of the Bengali People, Early Phase) in Bengali. Reprint. Kolkata: Pashcimbanga Niraksharata Durikaran Samity (Society for Eradication of Illiteracy, West Bengal), 1980.
58. Sarkar, Jadunath (ed): *History of Bengal,* Reprint, Patna 1973.
59. Sen, Sudipta. *The Empire of Free Trade.* Philadelphia: University of Pennsylvania Press, 1998.
60. Sinha, N.K. *Economic History of Bengal ; From Plassey to Permanent Settlement,* Vol. 1 & 2, Calcutta: Firma. K.L. Mukhopadhyay, 1961 & 1962.
61. Stein, Burton. *Vijayanagar: New Cambridge History of India* 1.2. Orient Longman, 1988.
62. Subrahmanyam, Sanjay. *The Political Economy of Commerce in South India,* 1550–1650. C.U.P., 1990.
63. Vilar, Pierre. *A History of Gold and Money.* N.L.B. 1976.
64. Yule, Henry and Burnell, A.C.: *Hobson-Jobson: A Glossary of Anglo-Indian Words and Phrases and Kindred Terms.* Delhi : Munshiram Manoharlal, 1976.

Index

ERRATA

Page	*Line*	*Printed*	*Actual*
Contents	11	Decean	Deccan
Preface	3	Majimdar	Majumdar
Preface	20	Gupts	Gupta
18	10	India	Indian
27	15	widspread	widespread
28	10	experimants	experiments
28	11	discorder	disorder
33	23	impse	impose
38	5	have	has
43	20	From	In
47	7	on	of
55	6	rold	role
55	12	pricer	place
57	14	even	ever
59	14	merchangs	merchants
59	25	and	any
61	12	on	one
61	28	prices	princes
61	34	the	be
62	2	rulers	ruler
65	36	meed	meet
66	8	merchaants	merchants
68	19	Marchants	Merchants
69	22	does	should
69	22	interpred	interpret
81	20	18	17–th
83	23 & 26	ration	ratio
87	26	prominant	prominent
93	36	precous	precious
96	38	bank. The	bank, the
101	4	this worlds	these words
104	35	Mushidabad	Murshidabad
129	9	puchanses	purchases
132	19	Companies	Company's
135	3	poer	power
137	24	advantage	benefit
143	3	Bangal	Bengal
147	33	mechandise	merchandise
148	20	puirchase	purchase
164	25	moted	noted
167	16	influenced	imposed
169	37	ole	old

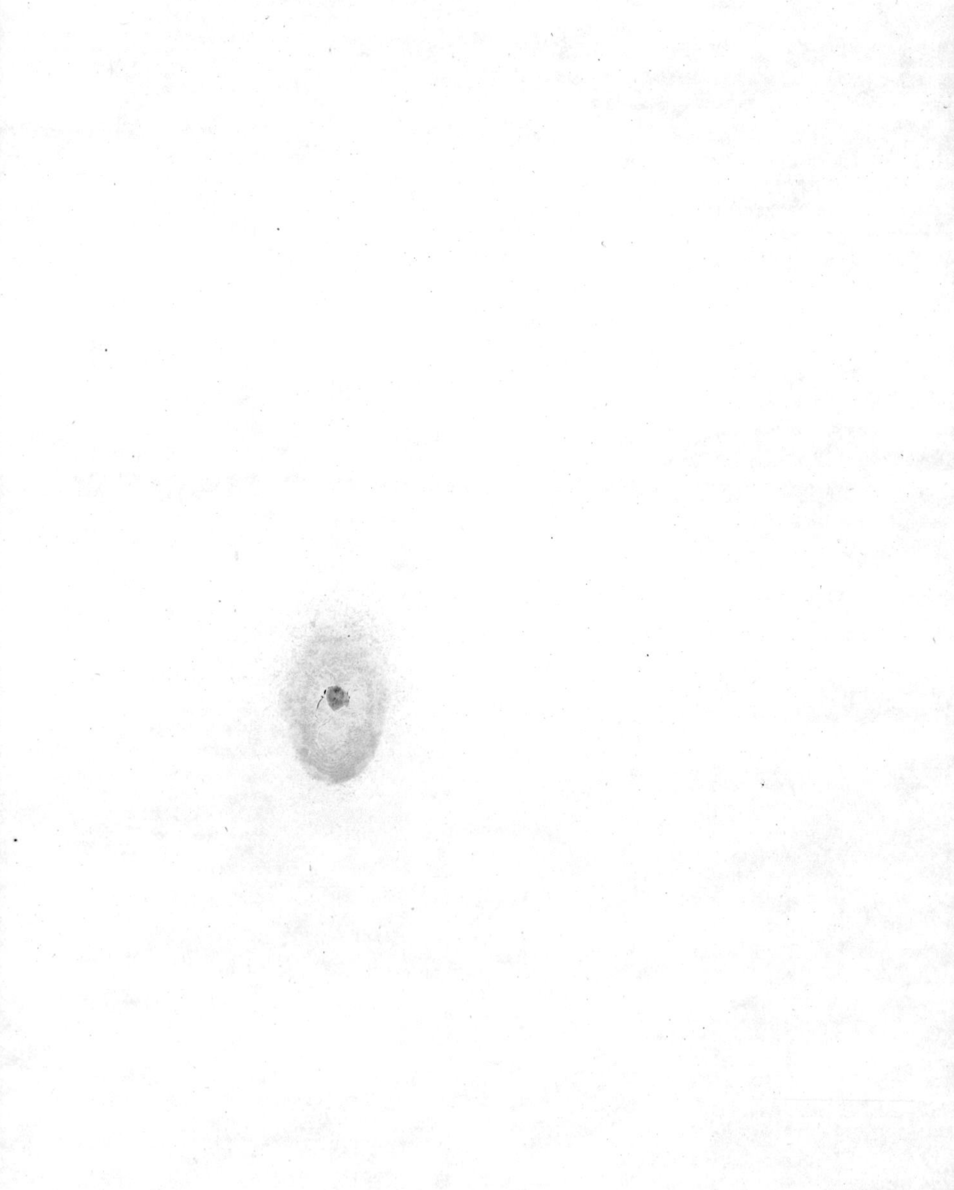